7-22-75

THE BRITISH ECONOMY
IN THEORY AND PRACTICE

THE BRITISH ECONOMY IN THEORY AND PRACTICE

JAMES M. LIVINGSTONE

ST. MARTIN'S PRESS   NEW YORK

AFFILIATED PUBLISHERS: Macmillan Limited, London –
also at Bombay, Calcutta, Madras and Melbourne

CONTENTS

PART I

THE ECONOMIC SYSTEM IN THEORY AND PRACTICE

There is no shortage of books on economics. Many, unfortunately, do not explain very clearly what goes on in the everyday world. They achieve logical precision often at the expense of moving further and further into economic theory and away from real-life conditions. This book attempts to tilt the balance the other way – to discuss current economic and political issues first, and then to consider whether the available theory explains what actually happens. It is therefore a book about an economy, the British economy, and how it functions, sloppily, not too efficiently perhaps in pure economic terms but by and large to the satisfaction of the general public.

The book is intended to be of use to a student who is looking for an overall, but hardly detailed, view of how the economy actually works : possibly for the businessman who has to cope with the vagaries of apparently arbitrary changes in government policy : and even for the politician or aspiring politician who has a somewhat simplistic view of what can be achieved in a democratic society.

Part I and particularly Chapter 1 contain sufficient of a theoretical economic framework for the general discussion which follows. The framework is not in the least sophisticated in terms of modern theory. Many economists would argue that it is not all that adequate to give structure to what otherwise might seem an amorphous mass of issues and problems. Chapters 2 and 3 introduce real-life qualifications, and attempt to relate the theory to historical situations.

Some readers will not previously have studied any economics : a proportion may be studying or have studied the subject fairly formally perhaps for a professional examination : others will have a good grasp of macro-economic theory. The layout of the book tries to cater for all these categories.

The complete beginner should read Chapter 1 with some care, even if he may feel at times that it is too theoretical to have much connection with what really goes on in the economy. The reader who is in some doubt about how much economic theory he has learnt or still remembers might start by reading the summary at the end of Chapter 1. If the points made in that summary seem self-evident, this chapter on economic theory can be omitted: if the points made are recognisable but not intellectually accept-able, he should bear in mind that what is being presented is not a logically watertight model but something more rough and ready, representing the degree of sophistication at which many national economic decisions are probably made, simply because the poli-ticians who have eventually to make the decisions tend to do so on very rough and ready criteria. If he is still unconvinced he might find that the qualifications introduced in the second chapter are more acceptable. Finally the reader who has a good grasp of economic theory might wish to go directly to the second part of the book, which discusses economic objectives and how they have to be modified in practice.

CHAPTER 1

A MODEL OF THE ECONOMY

THIS section is intended to build up a working model of an economy which bears some resemblance to Britain in the 1970s. It starts on a very simple scale, so simple indeed as to be virtually a caricature, and a series of very loose definitions. Modifications are then made to the first very crude model, and at the same time the definitions are given rather more precision until at the end of the section the reader will be presented with a systematically laid-out model, which, however grotesquely simplified, does parallel what actually happens in the British economy.

The First Stage – An Economy without Government

Let us imagine an economy of perhaps one million inhabitants engaged in occupations from which they derive their living. This community has no government, and therefore no taxation, social security or any other activity of this nature; it has no trade or any other economic connection with any other part of the world, i.e. it is a closed system in which neither goods nor purchasing power can leak out of the economy; and, a final simplification, all the goods it produces are also consumed during the year, i.e. there are no stocks of goods or materials which are carried over from one year to another.

Merely to list these limitations illustrates what an artificially simple model this stage is so far. There are in practice still more unrealistic assumptions lurking under the surface, but they can be tackled once, so to speak, the model has begun to work.

To give a touch of reality let us suppose that this community of one million produces £1000 million of goods and services annually, or about £1000 of goods and services per head of the population: this is about the output per head of the British economy, so, however artificial the conditions of the model, it represents an economy with about the present standard of living in Britain.

Given the assumptions already made about the closed economy we can look at the economic activity of this community in three separate ways: as *national expenditure*, i.e. £1000 million of purchasing power available to buy all the goods and services being produced by the community during the year; as *national output*, i.e. £1000 million of goods and services being created during the year; and finally as *national income*, i.e. £1000 million of income being made available to members of the community because they are producing or trading in these goods and services.

Within the very limiting restrictions we have imposed, these three measures in this closed community, namely national expenditure, national output and national income, are different ways of looking at the same economic activity; and in theory it ought to be possible to estimate the value of each of the three measures separately and come up with the same total of £1000 millions.

National Expenditure, National Output, National Income

So far the definitions of the three measures have been very loose indeed, but they can now be spelt out in a little more detail.

(a) *National Expenditure.* The main point of normal expenditure – spending – is simply consumer satisfaction: the housewife buys food, the family buys clothing and shelter, either by paying rent or purchasing a house; some people will buy more expensive consumer goods, passenger cars for example. Consumer satisfaction in this sense includes not merely physical goods, but services, i.e. travel by rail or air normally involves buying a service, not a train or an aircraft.

But although our consumer needs are virtually insatiable, not everybody spends his or her income to the last penny every year. People save money for various reasons. This means presumably that they envisage spending their present income on consumer goods and services at some future date. The immediate effect, however, is that so far as the community is concerned, *most* purchasing power is spent each year but *some* is not spent, or at least not spent on consumer goods. The quantity of purchasing power not spent is 'saved'. Savings in this context are not quite what are normally thought of as savings: possibly 'hoarding' is nearer the mark, although this is a rather loaded word in everyday usage.

It is likely that only a small fraction of this available purchasing power will be saved. Again reverting to reality, in Britain in recent years savings have been about 8 per cent of the purchasing power available.

(b) *National output* means the total value of goods and services produced in the community, for which money payment is made or whose value can be estimated. The products will once again include not merely physical goods, but services. Producing cars or cabbages, or cleaning a house for payment, all are the result of productive work in this sense and all add to the money value of national output. The reader will probably see snags in defining exactly what is paid work in this context but the principle is easy enough to grasp even if the exact definition gets rather fuzzy.

At this stage it is worth noting that the community is almost certainly producing goods and services which do not give any obvious immediate consumer satisfaction. Three examples of consumer goods and services have been quoted, passenger cars, cabbages and cleaning a house for payment. But as well as producing consumer goods and services of this sort the economy will also produce, say, lorries or tractors, not merely passenger cars; industrial crops like jute as well as edible products; and factories need to be cleaned without there being much obvious consumer satisfaction created. These types of goods and services which are vital in a community, but do not give immediate consumer satisfaction, can be defined as capital goods and services. In general it can be said of capital goods and services that they make the production of future consumer goods and services easier but do not give immediate satisfaction.

(c) *National income* means the sum total of all the incomes which arise in the community from these activities; most obviously perhaps in the form of wages. Most people in a modern economy are employees. For others, say small shopkeepers working for themselves, the income will come from self-employment. Yet others in the community who own businesses, or farms, hire out land or lend money, will receive incomes in the form of profits, rents, interest and so on.

The situation may not be as clear-cut as all that. Taking again the three examples of cabbages, cars and cleaning, the production of these goods and services could produce incomes which could be defined under various headings. To the self-employed farmer the production and sale of cabbages would be an income from self-employment; to a farm worker a wage; to the owner of the land the farmer utilised, his share of the income would appear as rent. As far as manufacturing cars was concerned money income would accrue in various forms – as wages for an assembly-line worker; income, profit or a salary to the car salesman, depending partly on his status, partly on how he viewed his own occupation; to the owner of shares in the car-making company as dividends. Finally, so far as the house-cleaning activity was concerned, if a charwoman was employed directly by the house-owner, this would represent a wage, if cleaning services were supplied by a company, wages, dividends, profits – any or all might accrue.

In a real-life economy, how the cake representing national income is sliced up depends in part at least on the political set-up of the society. Implicitly in this first crude model, since there is no government, and therefore presumably no state activity, the means of production are in private hands. Incomes including wages from employment or self-employment, dividends and profits from ownership or control of the means of production i.e. capital goods, factories, firms of all sorts, or rent from the ownership of land are all possible. In theory they could be sorted out and listed under various headings: in practice they would be jumbled together and scarcely distinguishable.

A Summary Thus Far

On the present very fuzzy definitions of the three aspects of national product as expenditure, output and income we have obviously begged a number of questions, but the nub of the issue is that these definitions involved activities where goods and services are valued, bought and sold in money terms: we have essentially three different ways of looking at, and measuring, economic activity in a community which already bears a resemblance to the British economy; and in the last analysis the three concepts are one and the same.

We can summarise the information, particularly that contained in (a) and (b) above, in the following two statements (or more strictly, equations):

(1) National expenditure   = consumption + savings

(2) National product   = goods and services which give immediate consumer satisfaction + capital goods and services

So far as equation (2) is concerned we can now be more precise about what is meant by capital goods and services. Briefly the latter can be thought of as anything which does not give immediate satisfaction to the purchaser, but will probably increase satisfaction later on because the producer will be able to produce rather more. If a factory owner spends money in buying a new machine for his factory instead of buying himself a new car for his private use or going on an expensive holiday, he gets no immediate satisfaction; on the other hand the capital expenditure on the new machine probably means more production and a higher income in the future – and possibly the prospect of buying a more expensive car or of a more luxurious holiday in a year or two.

The extent of spending on capital goods (known in this context as *investment*) significantly affects the rate at which an economy grows. This is a point to which we will return, but for the moment the reader should take note of the term 'investment', as meaning expenditure on capital goods and services. This is not quite the normal meaning of 'investment' which conjures up visions of buying shares on the Stock Exchange. Indeed, as we shall see, a particular problem about economics is that many of the terms, e.g. savings and investment, have a rather different meaning than that in everyday use.

Defining the Equations more Closely

Equation (1) says that national expenditure = consumption + savings. In the conventional lettering of economics this can be shortened to

$$Y = C + S$$

where Y = national expenditure (or, using the general term, national product);

C = consumption; and

S = savings.

All that this says however is that people in the community either spend their current income or don't spend it. This somewhat banal conclusion arises because we have defined money not spent by consumers as savings. The point has already been made that the term 'savings' is not being used in quite its everyday sense, which is roughly money put into a bank. In the very simple model of the closed economy we are making no assumptions about how savings are handled in practice. It does not matter for the moment whether they are being put into banks or even kept under the mattress – all that matters at present is that they are not being spent to give immediate consumer satisfaction.

The point has already been made that savings in a country like Britain are at the present about 8 per cent of national expenditure. Some other countries save a much greater proportion, others much less. It might be of some interest to consider briefly what causes variations in the proportion of savings.

Obviously every individual in a community has his own ideas on what proportion of his income he will save. Some common-sense assumptions can be made however. Thus a poor person will find it more difficult to save than a rich one. A comparatively poor community will find it more difficult to save than a wealthy one. Moreover the wealthier that individuals or nations become, the more they will save, not only in *absolute* but also in *relative* terms. To put it at its simplest, with an annual income of perhaps £100 an individual might manage to save only a penny in every pound, or even nothing at all because he had to spend virtually everything on the very necessities of life. But if his income increased tenfold to £1000 he would be unlikely to buy ten times as much necessities such as food. He might now find it relatively easy to save 10 per cent of his new income, i.e. £100 annually. If his income rose to £10,000 his tastes – and extravagances – would probably adjust rapidly but common sense suggests that he could save proportionately more. He might now save 15 to 20 per cent of his income without undue hardship, i.e. £1500 to £2000.

This is not, of course, an absolute rule applying in every instance. Tastes, as has been remarked, would change: some individuals would always spend income up to the last penny. But in spite of individual variations we might reasonably expect that in our model community of one million with an average income of £1000 there would be a fair proportion of saving; and if in time the community grew richer its proportion of saving would probably increase.

Equation (2) says

$$Y = C + I$$

where $Y =$ national output, i.e. national product,
$C =$ consumer goods and
$I =$ investment or capital goods.

The reader may feel that we have glossed over any distinctions between the definition of C in equation (1) and equation (2). But one of our assumptions was that everything which was consumed in the year was produced in the year and C, whether defined as consumption or as output of consumer goods, means the same in our very limited model.

Savings and Investment

From the equations

$$Y = C + S$$

and

$$Y = C + I$$

we can deduce that $S = I$, i.e. the amount of savings (purchasing power not spent on consumer goods) = the amount invested in capital equipment – at first sight a shattering glimpse of the obvious. But this is not as obvious a point as it might seem. What *appears* to be common sense is the idea that if we want to spend money on capital equipment, whether it be a factory, a hand tool, a road, or anything else, we must first save to pay for it. More precisely perhaps *somebody* in the community must be saving so that somebody else can borrow the money to pay for capital goods.

It is important to be quite clear on this point. The probability is that, even in our simple closed community, if somebody wishes to spend money on a good deal of capital equipment, then he will have to use other people's savings as well as his own. A banking system exists to make this easier, i.e. to assist the translation of the savings in our restricted definition of virtual hoarding to the everyday meaning of the term. If people's savings are put through a banking system instead of being hoarded, then bigger capital projects, i.e. larger-scale investment, can be made than if every individual, or even every firm, had to make its own savings before investing.

It costs money to borrow money – hence the concept of interest. The rate of interest provides a link between savings and investment. That last statement is not quite the same as saying that the rate of interest is the only, or even necessarily the most important, link but it is very easy to make this assumption.

The *common-sense* but, as we shall see, dangerously over-simplified concept is that savings precede investment, and that the two are kept in balance by interest rates. If more is being saved than is being invested, the argument runs, then more people are willing to lend than to borrow. As a result interest rates fall, people are less willing to save while more investment becomes an economic proposition, and borrowing picks up until savings and investment balance. The mechanism works in reverse too. Heavy investment means heavy borrowing, increased interest rates attract more savings and discourage some investment, so that once again a balance is struck.

A good deal of economic policy in the nineteenth century and first three decades of the twentieth century turned on a rather more sophisticated version of this. By the 1930s, however, it had become apparent that with economic stagnation and mass unemployment almost a permanent feature of western society, there was something wrong with the assumptions.

An inordinate amount could be written introducing various qualifications but the shortcomings of the orthodox savings/investment relationship can be summed up fairly briefly.

On the *savings* side one has to consider why people save. They may do so for very specific reasons, for a holiday, to buy a car, to put down a deposit for a house : or even simply 'for a rainy day'. That last cliché contains an important truth. People may save as a precaution against an uncertain future : in this situation the amount of interest they are being paid is certainly a factor, but it is not necessarily the most important factor. An obvious example of this is behaviour during an economic recession or depression. Some people will save less, simply because they have lost their jobs and incomes; but even in the most severe depression most people still have their jobs, and this great majority who are still in employment are more likely than not to save more than usual in case they in their turn lose their jobs. If an individual is saving because he is afraid of losing his job, a drop in interest rates will not change his behaviour very much.

Equally why do people *borrow*? Partly, of course, the cost of the borrowing does matter. Common sense again suggests that the potential borrower must expect to make more out of investing in capital equipment than he has to pay by way of interest. But at least as important as the cost of borrowing is the expectation the individual has of future developments. If he expects the national economy to prosper he is likely to want to increase his stock of capital equipment or personal possessions, and will therefore be ready to borrow. If he expects a depression he will not borrow – regardless of how cheaply he could do so. Expectation rather than rates of interest matter, because both from the savings and the borrowing points of view they are self-fulfilling prophecies. If enough individuals are convinced that economic conditions are going to get worse, and as a result save money instead of spending or delay investment until better times, then economic conditions will indeed get worse as the demand for products falls away. The individual industrialist or wage-earner acts rationally in his own interests but the overall effect is to produce the very economic recession he fears. What is good for the individual is not, in this case, good for the community.

The self-fulfilling prophecy also acts in the reverse direction, to create boom conditions, although probably not so decisively as in the other direction. Optimism and the economic decisions it breeds produce, or at least make more likely, expansion.

The importance of general optimism or pessimism – expectations in modern jargon – was implicitly appreciated in the nineteenth and early twentieth centuries. Unfortunately, there was another fairly explicit assumption which tended to mask some of the consequences. This was the assumption that depressions, however induced, tended to cure themselves, that there was in effect a built-in stabilising mechanism in the system which ironed out temporary aberrations. At its simplest, the argument could be summarised thus : even if people acted in their own interests during a depression and by so doing exaggerated the process, nevertheless within a comparatively short time the situation had to improve. Initially stocks of goods, capital or consumer, would be cut back. But in a relatively short time, even at the lower level of activity, stocks would be run down faster than they were being replaced, interest rates would fall until the point came when it would be worth while to expand production again and to replenish depleted stocks. Employment would begin to rise and the whole economic climate would alter for the better as the conviction of better times ahead took root.

The acceptance of what might be called the classical savings investment relationship through interest rates assumed that the normal situation was prosperity and full employment. There was really no logical reason, however, to make that really vital additional assumption. What destroyed most of the belief in the classical savings/investment relationship was an awareness that in the 1930s depression and high unemployment rates (and cheap money, i.e. low interest rates) had been the situation for a very long time. There was no reason any more to suppose that full employment of manpower and resources was normal, any more than that heavy unemployment and unused capacity were normal. Full employment, the so-called normal situation, was beginning to look like only one possible condition out of an almost infinite variety of possible conditions. What was needed in fact was a general theory explaining the behaviour of national product, employment levels, etc., and showing how one particular condition (in this case full employment) could be achieved without having to wait for it to come round again by chance, so to speak.

The Keynesian Approach to Savings and Investment

The general theory which emerged in the 1930s was largely the work of J. M. Keynes, later Lord Keynes, probably the most influential economist of the twentieth century. What follows here is a simplefied version of the relevant portion of his work – and it is well to remember that simplification inevitably implies some distortion. Moreover, though the Keynesian approach has been modified and indeed seriously challenged over nearly four decades since it was first expounded, it remains a remarkably useful tool to illustrate the workings of an economy. We shall have to look at objections and qualifications later on, but at the moment we shall apply the Keynesian approach rather uncritically to our first simple model.

Briefly Keynes argued that the level of investment determined the level of national income, employment and thus growth. Too little investment would produce underutilisation of resources, heavy unemployment and slow growth : the appropriate level of investment would produce full employment – which was the key aspect of the problem when he produced his theory in the mid 1930s. Too much investment would produce over-full employment and its other consequences would be inflation and a runaway boom. The intriguing point which appeared to explain away the hitherto inexplicable stable unemployment of the early 1930s was that any level of investment could produce a stable condition : in other words if unemployment and underutilisation of resources existed in a community the situation need not automatically cure itself, by a return to an imaginary norm of full employment.

In the light of this concept let us look at the equations again, this time reversing their order to consider the aspects of national output as $Y = C + I$.

What are the characteristics of the right-hand side of the equation, namely consumer goods and investment (i.e. capital goods)? Briefly we can say that there is a really important difference between C and I in that the production of consumer goods not merely results in the creation of purchasing power, in the form of wages, profits, rents, dividends and so on, but that the consumer goods themselves mop up the community's purchasing power. The output of capital goods likewise produces purchasing power but these goods do not mop up purchasing power immediately in terms of consumer satisfaction because people do not normally buy such items as tractors, factories, machine tools and the like for the personal satisfaction they get from buying consumer goods.

The situation, of course, is not that simple. The more investment (i.e. production of capital goods and services) an economy experiences in a year, the greater will be its potential to produce yet more consumer goods in the future, with its increased capacity; but at the moment our primary concern is with the point that investment creates purchasing power for individuals without simultaneously creating consumer goods and services to satisfy this extra purchasing power. Investment in this sense *injects* purchasing power into the economy : in our present simple model of a closed economy it is the only way of injecting more purchasing power.

If, on the other hand, we look at our equation $Y = C + S$ and consider what we mean by 'saving' in the context, it becomes apparent that saving in this limited sense drains purchasing power out of the economy, i.e. it is a *leakage*, again the only leakage in our present model.

In summary, in our present very simple model investment injects purchasing power into the economy, saving leaks it out.

If there is more investment than saving, the short-term effect is to mop up any available stocks of consumer goods and encourage more to be produced : if for any reason they cannot be produced fast enough, then the price of the available consumer goods will rise, i.e. there will be a tendency towards inflation.

If more is being saved than is being invested the fall in purchasing power available means that consumption falls, so probably do prices, i.e. deflation appears.

We have now introduced two more very important concepts, inflation and deflation. Most people know vaguely what the terms mean even if they would find it hard to define them. Let us at the moment stick to a very rough-and-ready definition which follows from what has been written above. Inflation means too much purchasing power chasing too few goods, particularly consumer goods. Deflation means too little purchasing power to mop up available goods. There is perhaps another nuance to these terms to be noted – the idea that inflation is 'bad', but unplanned, but that deflation, also 'bad', is a deliberate policy. Like any other definition so far introduced these two will have to be tightened up; for the moment, however, they will suffice.

The Multiplier

At this point it will be convenient to introduce one of the more powerful tools in modern economics, the concept of the multiplier, a systematic treatment of the hitherto rather vague concepts of injections and leakages.

In our simple model of a closed economy without government we gave a touch of reality by adding actual figures – a million inhabitants, national product of £1000 million. Let us now add one more figure about consumption and savings, namely to assume that on average the population spend about 92 per cent of current incomes and save 8 per cent, i.e. £920 million of national expenditure goes on consumption and £80 million is saved.

There is incidentally nothing particularly significant about the figures except that 8 per cent saving is about the level currently achieved in the U.K. economy: in this respect at least the model is not wildly out of touch with real life, however remote it may be in other aspects.

The figures 92 per cent consumption and 8 per cent saving can be expressed as ratios, namely 0.92 and 0.08. At this point we can now introduce two useful terms to describe these ratios, namely the average propensity to consume and the average propensity to save. In this instance

$$APC = 0.92$$
$$APS = 0.08$$

By definition, in our closed economy, the two average propensities must add up to one, because consumption and savings are the only possible means of disposing of purchasing power.

Now let us suppose that in this economy someone introduces an extra £1000 of investment, possibly by building an extension to a factory. Since this is an extra investment, £1000 of extra purchasing power is going to be injected into the economy in a fairly short time – as wages to the building workers, possibly also as profits and dividends to the building firm, the suppliers of raw materials, etc. What happens to the extra £1000 extra purchasing power?

At first sight we might assume that it will be consumed and saved in the same ratio as expressed in the average propensities to consume and save already given. But to revert to a point already made, the richer an individual or nation, the more readily he or it saves, not only in absolute but in relative terms.

This gives rise to two more useful terms, namely the marginal propensity to consume and the marginal propensity to save (MPC and MPS). These simply mean the proportions of extra income which are consumed or saved. Again, as in the case of the average propensities in our closed economy, the marginal propensities add up to unity. Although the average propensity is the easier concept to grasp, the marginal propensity is in practice the more important.

In the relatively well-off community it might well be that of

the extra £1000 of purchasing power created by the new investment £900 goes on current expenditure by its recipients and
£100 is saved. In this case

$$MPC = 0.9$$
$$MPS = 0.1$$

Thus we have £1000 extra purchasing power of which £900
is spent on consumer goods and £100 is saved. But this is not
the end of the process. The £900 has created a demand for consumer goods as the money passes over the shop counter, so to
speak, and therefore means an extra £900 purchasing power in
the economy. If this in turn is spent and saved in the MPC and
MPS proportions then 0.9 of the £900, i.e. £810, will be spent
and the remaining £90 will be saved: this £810 extra purchasing power goes the same way and so on.

It is easier to see the implications in the form of a table:

TABLE I

Extra income (from investment)	Extra consumption (MPC = 0·9)	Extra savings (MPS = 0·1)
£1000	£900	£100
£900	£810	£90
£810	£729	£81
£729	£656·1	£72·9
	and so on	
£10,000	£9000	£1000

This is a series whose terms could go on to infinity. In practice
after ten or fifteen rounds the effects have largely run their
course. But the point is that the sum to infinity gives the totals for
*extra income, extra consumption and extra savings as £10,000,
£9000 and £1000 respectively.* If the arithmetically dubious
reader is prepared to sit down and work out the figures
for succeeding rounds a few minutes of simple division and
addition will convince him that the totals are going to come out
at this and in fact have been very nearly reached after ten to
fifteen rounds because the extra volume in the succeeding rounds
has become smaller and smaller.

In our example the original investment has had a multiple effect – in this case a tenfold effect. The original £1000 of investment has produced £10,000 of extra income before its effects are exhausted : this includes £9000 of extra consumption and £1000 of saving. Not the least intriguing aspect of this investment multiplier is the final savings figure which exactly equals the original investment. Here indeed the common-sense assumption that savings precede investment has been reversed : investment here has created savings.

The reader is invited to check that this result follows for other marginal propensities to consume and save, for example $MPC = 0.8$ and $MPS = 0.2$. In this instance the multiplier effect will turn out to be five-fold, but once again the end result is that savings equal the original investment.

What determines the size of the multiplier? In the worked example, the multiplier was 10 : in that suggested for working out by the reader it is 5. The multiplier is in fact

$$\frac{1}{MPS} \quad \text{or} \quad \frac{1}{1 - MPC}$$

In words, it is the reciprocal of the marginal propensity to save. The smaller the proportion of extra income which is saved by the community, the greater will be the multiplier effect. Another way of putting the same point is that the more purchasing power that is saved or 'leaked out' of the series at each round, the smaller will be the multiplier effect.

The elegance of this particular concept becomes apparent when applied to our closed economic system with no government. What is implied by the multiplier concept is a more precise statement of a point made earlier, that, depending on the level of investment existing in the community, there can be an infinite variety of levels of national income and hence of employment. It ought therefore to be possible in theory at least to choose a level of investment which created a high level of national income and full employment.

Ignoring for the moment the obvious point that, in the present model of the economy there is no government which might be able to settle the 'right' level of investment for full employment, it becomes clear that, in a situation of underemployment and underutilisation of national resources, the more investment can be increased the higher the level of national product and the lower the level of unemployment will become. This move will have the added bonus that increased investment as well as increasing employment today will, by creating more capital equipment, make the economy a richer one in the future.

There is no theoretical limit to this model; there is a very practical real-life limitation. National product presumably has some sort of limit, once we approach full utilisation of all the community's resources, including human resources. What happens to the multiplier effect when it has mopped up all the spare resources, when we have 'full employment', whatever that means? The short answer is that national product will continue to respond to increased investment. But the rise in national product or national income will be in money terms only, not *real* increases in output. After the point of 'full employment' increased investment produces not more output, but inflation. It would be very convenient if we could assume that increased investment produced increased employment up to the point of full employment and then, and only then, inflation. In fact inflation is likely to set in fairly rapidly even when there is 2, 3 or more per cent of the available work force still unemployed.

To revert to a real-life situation is complicated because there are problems of defining full employment – and these problems can only be discussed in detail later on. But even so, it is possible to pinpoint actual estimates in the British economy which marked the watershed when the incipient inflation began to outweigh the advantages of more and more employment. For historical reasons, practical full employment at the end of the Second World War was deemed to involve about 3 per cent unemployment. This estimate might have seemed incredibly optimistic compared with the inter-war years when unemployment on occasion was over 10 per cent. But in the immediate post-war period 3 per cent proved too high to be politically acceptable and the rate went down to about 1 per cent with inevitable inflationary consequences.

It would be convenient to be able to quote a generally agreed rate of unemployment which would have been politically and economically acceptable as a price of containing inflation. No such figure was available however and indeed, even if it had been available for any one time, it might have been irrelevant a few years later. In the 1950s, for example, unemployment was generally well under the 3 per cent ideal of the immediate post-war period, without inflation being excessive : in the early 1970s however there were occasions when excessive inflation existed in harness with over 3 per cent unemployment. If, at the latter period there was a theoretical level of unemployment which would have cured inflation rapidly it was a level which was just not politically or morally acceptable to either of the major political parties.

The Complication of Stockholding

So far for the sake of simplicity it has been assumed that the consumer goods and capital goods which are being produced are being used up more or less as soon as they are available, and that by implication the exact ratio of consumer to capital goods is produced. But it would be more realistic to think of the situation where the economy generates stocks of goods, finished consumer goods, work in progress, even raw materials which have been made available but which have yet to appear in the shape of components to consumer or capital products.

If however we apply our definition of investment as anything which produces purchasing power to producers without immediately creating the means to satisfy the increased purchasing power, it becomes clear that it would be reasonable to include the creation of stocks, including undistributed consumer goods, as being akin to or possibly a part of investment. Investment therefore includes not merely the manufacture of capital goods but also of stocks whether consumer or capital, the consumer goods coming within the definition as long as they are not released to the distribution system.

Savings and Investment in the United Kingdom

It was noted earlier that savings in the United Kingdom tend to be about 8 per cent of national expenditure. It might seem reasonable therefore to assume that investment would be about the same – or slightly more if there was growth in the national economy with savings tending to equal investment. In reality, however, investment is about 18 per cent, which suggests that either our model is completely out of touch with reality or that there is very rapid growth in the economy – and very rapid inflation – or that the balance of injections and leakages contains rather more than the two so far discussed. We can now add another form of injection and another form of leakage.

The Second Stage – A Closed Economy with Government

The next stage in bringing realism into the model is to introduce the factor of a government, whose activities, particularly economic activities, will complicate the situation. In an economy like Britain, the government is responsible for about 50 per cent of all economic activity; in wartime it may account for much more than that.

By implication in the original model without government all economic activities were in the hands of private individuals or companies. Now at this second stage there will be a public sector to the economy as well as a private sector. The public sector comprises not merely the everyday activities of government but also the economic activities of companies or corporations owned by the state, which are run on commercial or semi-commercial lines. In this context therefore government includes not only the state activities of the central government but also the local government functions, and the sort of commercial or semi-commercial activities involved include nationalised industries and public utilities such as electricity and gas. Like privately owned companies they will charge for services although they do not necessarily operate on the same commercial principles as private companies.

The effects of having a government in the model can be looked at from two aspects: the government *spends* money and *collects* money in the form of taxes, loans, receipts from nationalised industries, etc.

Public expenditure may be for a variety of purposes and the implications vary according to these.

(*a*) Expenditure on power stations, bridges, railways, aircraft, for nationalised industries, etc., expenditure which is virtually indistinguishable from investment on capital goods as already defined in the first stage. This is public investment in its strictest sense.

(*b*) Expenditure on roads and schools, infirmaries, police services, etc., whose effects are broadly similar to the first category in that ultimately they give consumer satisfaction but some time in the future. There is no very clear division between (*a*) and (*b*) except that there is a commercial element in the first group, i.e. people will eventually pay directly for services provided, e.g. power, travel facilities, etc., whereas in the latter the services are generally provided free to the individual user in the sense that the services are not paid for directly by the individual user but indirectly by taxation, which is not specifically levied for that purpose, i.e. there is no hospital tax, education tax, etc., which varies according to how much an individual uses the particular service.

(*c*) Expenditure on defence: this is overwhelmingly expenditure which is not likely to produce consumer satisfaction in any conventional sense. Defence expenditure is not particularly an economic activity but necessarily is determined by other factors. In some respects however expenditure of this sort produces results which, in their immediate effects, are rather similar to public sector investment. Production of the goods and services for defence produces purchasing power in the form of wages, profits, etc., but no corresponding consumer satisfaction.

(*d*) Various types of expenditure can be classified as 'transfers' of purchasing power. They are not pre-emptive claims on national resources in quite the same sense as the earlier groups; instead this group of expenditures is intended to transfer purchasing power from one section of the community to the other. The most obvious example is government expenditure on pensions which are intended to benefit the less well-off section of the community, the retired or the incapacitated. Other examples of transfers might be subsidies to particular groups, e.g. public housing at low rents, rent rebates, payments to nationalised industries to enable them to provide goods and services to the public at a price below their true cost, or to prevent redundancies.

(*e*) Finally, there is a group including loans, payments of interest on loans, or outright gifts which again transfer income from one section of the community to others.

There has been no hard and fast division between the various groups and there is an element of arbitrariness about the classification. But what does emerge is that these are two major results of this public sector expenditure. The first is any activity which involves a claim on national resources, or which pre-empts resources to public sector use. About 30 per cent of all British production is covered by this category. The other activity is of the 'transfer' variety which merely reallocates resources between one sector of the community and another. It is of course possible that any government expenditure may include elements of both.

It is the first type of government expenditure with which we are primarily concerned. The point is that whether this type of expenditure is exactly equivalent to investment in adding to national wealth, as in general groups (a) and (b); or whether it is necessary for other reasons, e.g. external or internal security or health, where, however necessary, it does not really add to the stock of capital equipment in a country, then the immediate effect is largely the same as for investment, i.e. it creates purchasing power for the producers without immediately providing consumer satisfaction, so there is a multiplier effect.

The second type of government expenditure is not, in general, likely to have the same multiplier effects – though this statement may have to be qualified slightly.

Taxation, loans and government receipts are the other side of the coin. If governments spend money, they must also take steps to control purchasing power. The main source is in the form of taxation (including local rates). But it will also be possible for the government to borrow, just as private individuals and companies do : indeed the government will be able to borrow more easily than anyone else.

The main instrument of government taxation is the Budget, normally an annual event. Although local government taxation is also important, it is closely integrated with central government policy and will not be treated separately.

The main purpose of the Budget is to raise revenue by taxation to meet most of the proposed expenditure by the state. At a deeper level, however, what is involved is not so much the amount of money taken in taxes, etc., but the proportion of national resources which is being pre-empted by the public sector.

A secondary purpose of the Budget and related legislation is to deal with the problem of transfer payments, i.e. the Budget is an instrument to reallocate national income, not merely by the positive allocation of purchasing power to the less well-off sections of the community, but also negatively by affecting the allocating of purchasing power through the incidence of taxation. The government can decide which sections of the community are to be heavily taxed, which to be lightly taxed and so on.

It is not proposed to deal in detail with the implications of budgetary policy here. This will be a separate issue later on. But in the present context it is sufficient to note that the government can attempt to affect the rate of growth of the economy not only by deciding how much investment it decrees in the public sector, how much it encourages investment by the private sector by granting or denying tax concessions to companies who wish to increase their investment, but also by how it chooses to finance its own expenditure, i.e. by taxation or by borrowing.

In the past, a distinction was drawn between what was known as 'above the line' expenditure which, roughly, was the day-to-day necessities of government expenditure, and 'below the line' expenditure which was exceptional capital developments and emergency expenditures. The distinction was that 'above the line' expenditure was regarded as appropriately met from taxation, and the remainder by borrowing. A 'balanced' Budget was one which met the needs of everyday 'above the line' expenditure with neither a surplus nor a deficit. Some types of capital expenditure would normally be met by borrowing. The National Debt, which is the embodiment of 'below the line' expenditure in the past, arose in the eighteenth century when the wars of that period had become too expensive to be paid for out of taxation.

The terms 'above the line' and 'below the line' are no longer officially used and the distinction is in some respects conventional rather than precisely identifiable. Thus 'below the line' borrowing by the government gives rise to interest repayments which are presumably routine 'above the line' expenditure. In more general terms the distinction is an artificial one which the government can ignore – and increasingly in the last thirty or more years it has done so – to control demand. Thus if the government wanted to increase demand during a recession it might find it more convenient to cover part of its current expenditure by borrowing (*a*) because reduced taxation effectively increases disposable income to be spent by individuals or companies and so increases purchasing power and (*b*) in a recession, when, as we have seen, savings are likely to be rising while the private sector is reluctant to borrow, and public borrowing will be very desirable to counter the deflationary effects.

The converse is also true. When a runaway economic boom threatens to get out of control and produce unacceptable inflation, government expenditure based on increased taxation rather than on borrowing may have the effect of reducing the pressure of demand on the economy. This time, what is being pre-empted by the state is not so much more of the nation's resources as more of the nation's purchasing power.

If we consider the implications of the argument that if necessary the government can raise more by way of taxation than it requires for day-to-day expenditure, it becomes apparent that the distinction between taxation on the one hand and savings on the other can become blurred. Surplus budgeting is one device for restraining inflation because it means excess taxation, i.e. in effect a form of saving, forced rather than voluntary and by nature deflationary. The converse 'deficit budgeting' relies on borrowing to cover part of current expenditure and is a way of stimulating demand in a recession.

As the reader will no doubt suspect we can now consider the characteristics of taxation as being very similar to those of savings. They effectively take away purchasing power from the individual or company : they represent, like savings, a leakage. Just as savings was the obverse of investment, so taxation is the obverse of government expenditure, all four of these terms being used in their limited, not their everyday use.

For an equilibrium situation at the first stage of the model, investment had to equal savings, i.e. $I = S$. One could now argue in similar terms that government expenditure of the 'non-transfer' variety ought to equal taxation, i.e. $G = T$, where G and T represent government (i.e. public) expenditure and taxation respectively, again in the restricted sense defined. If G does not equal T, then the situation which we have described vaguely as surplus or deficit budgeting exists.

Since we are using the concepts of *injections* and *leakages*, i.e. the multiplier concept of public expenditure and taxation, it should be possible to develop average and marginal propensities equivalent to those for savings and consumption. The latter might be described as propensities to taxation and to disposable incomes. The reader should be able to satisfy himself that the size of the multiplier is inversely related to the marginal propensity to taxation, which is a somewhat elaborate way of saying that one way of containing inflation, in the short run, may be to take away purchasing power by increased taxation. In such a case taxation T might include an element of forced savings. Table 1 (p. 22) could be retitled Extra income (from public expenditure); Extra consumption (i.e. marginal disposable income after taxation); and Extra taxation (marginal tax rate). If the taxation were at the rate of 10p in the £, then the calculations would be the same as before, with a public expenditure multiplier of 10.

The two equations $I = S$ and $G = T$ can be added together. Thus in a closed economy the equation is $I + G = S + T$, i.e. private sector investment and those forms of government expenditure which create immediately unsatisfied consumer demand should equal savings by the private sector + taxation (again in our restricted sense). It should be noticed in passing that we have now slightly tightened up the definitions of $I = S$.

A very important point about this new equation of equilibrium is that the individual items on one side of the equation need not balance the equivalents on the other other side. As has been noted there is not a balance between investment and savings in the United Kingdom. Thus there is more room for manoeuvre in this enlarged equation than in either of the two originals. Now, according to the new situation, if a government wishes to raise national income or employment to a more acceptable level it has up to four lines of action.

(1) It may choose to encourage private investment (I).

(2) It may step up government expenditure (G).

(3) It could discourage private savings (S).

(4) It could reduce taxation (T).

Approaches (1) and (2) would induce a multiplier effect directly, approaches (3) and (4) would increase the size of the multiplier effect indirectly by reducing the leakages. As a matter of practical politics option (3) is unlikely to be used. It would almost certainly be impossible to put over a comparatively sophisticated economic point to the general public, without running the risk that when the time came to reverse the situation the public would think it was patriotic and profitable to save, although it had not been last month. The result is that even in

times of deficient demand when governments are trying frantically to reflate the economy, they are in effect compelled to stick
to a line on National Savings which is in the short run hampering
attempts to reflate the economy.

A brief aside on transfer payments. In our model we have
blurred round the question of what happens when a government
uses taxation as a method of taking purchasing power away from
one section of the community to give it to another. In general
these transfer payments are made on social or political grounds
and their economic effects are only a by-product. Obvious
examples of such socially motivated transfer payments are the
payment of retirement pensions to elderly and non-productive
members of society; or family allowances and various types of
subsidies which benefit one section of the community at the
expense of another.

Generally one would expect any deliberate transfer of purchasing power to be 'progressive' rather than 'regressive', i.e. it
is intended to spread purchasing power more equitably (however one defines this). Although politically a distinction is sometimes made between benefits which have been paid for by past
contributions and others which are paid as what used to be known
as Public Assistance, then National Assistance, it is from the
economic point of view relatively unimportant whether pensions
are paid for as a result of past contributions or not. Pensions and
benefits paid this year can only be met out of production this
year. Past contributions represented a useful 'leakage' in previous
years to limit claims on national resources, but do not help to
pay benefits out of the national resources currently available.

Finally, it was convenient as a first approximation to ignore
the economic effects of such socially motivated transfer payments.
In practice a transfer payment is rarely neutral in its economic
effects in the sense that it will probably increase consumption
fairly rapidly, since the less well-off sections of the community
who generally benefit from transfer payments have a higher
marginal propensity to consume, and so by reducing 'leakages'
increase the multiplier effect. Technically such payments are
likely to be 'demand rich'. Social security payments, even where
they are balanced by increased contributions elsewhere, are likely
immediately to increase overall consumption. If therefore our
equations were all that precise we would have to modify them to

take account of this; since however, like the actual running of the economy, the equations are very fuzzy indeed, it will be expedient merely to note the qualification and in practice ignore it as an individual economic effect.

The Third Stage – An Open Economy with Government

The next and final stage in creating this simple model of the economy is to take account of the fact that economies do not exist in isolation. No matter how nearly self-sufficient a nation is, its economic activities influence and are influenced by the existence of other economies. If anything, national economies are becoming more and more interdependent. A country like the United Kingdom, with its very substantial international economic links, in particular cannot realistically be treated in isolation.

If, then, our model is 'opened up' so to speak, what economic relationships are involved? There are several obvious ones. Trade – exports and imports; investment by foreigners in our economy and overseas investment by nationals of our own economy – here the term 'investment' is being used in a more usual sense, not merely in the somewhat restricted sense used so far; loans or gifts from one country to another; transfer of funds and property by individuals from one country to another and so on.

Exports and imports, the visible trade of the economist, are probably the most important.

Exports can be seen simply enough as involving a form of economic activity which creates income in the process of their manufacture, i.e. wages, profits, etc., and which thus creates purchasing power without simultaneously creating the means to satisfy that purchasing power, at least in so far as individuals in our economy are concerned since the goods themselves are not available in the economy. Exports are thus analogous in some of their effects to investment and government expenditure as defined earlier in the chapter, in that they create an injection of purchasing power within the economy. They have a multiplier effect, and it would be possible to develop an export multiplier, related average and marginal propensities and the like. Their effects will be the same as the two other types of injections we have already examined.

The concept of exports and the export multiplier can be seen at their most simple when goods are physically moved out of the

B

country. But there are other types of activities which can be classified as invisible exports. For example, a foreign tourist visiting Britain and spending money on hotels, sightseeing, etc., is producing substantially the same effects as if the services he is using were actually being exported. Some other services, films and television programmes exported might be more difficult to assess from the economic point of view, as would, for example, banking and insurance services provided by British financial institutions to be used by the rest of the world. The acid test, however, so far as we are concerned at the moment is the definition of those activities which create purchasing power in the economy without at the same time satisfying the extra purchasing power.

Imports are the other side of the coin. The reader will no doubt be able to apply the logic of the definitions. A leakage of purchasing power is anything which mops up purchasing without at the same time creating new jobs and purchasing power elsewhere in the economy. Imports, in this respect, have virtually the same effect as savings and taxation as defined earlier, with again the appropriate average and marginal propensities to import.

In the same way, apart from physical imports, there can be other activities, essentially movements in the opposite directions from invisible exports. These invisible imports include overseas spending by British tourists, etc., which have a leakage effect.

Thus it would be possible to envisage a very simple equation relating exports and imports as defined, which can either stand on their own or be added to the existing equation which is being built up. On its own the equation is simply Exports = Imports. Even in this simple form there are some very important implications:

(a) In *isolation*, i.e. assuming that there are no other injections or leakages, the implication is that an increase in exports will in time be balanced by an equivalent increase in imports. The process will work through the multiplier effect raising national income and employment. Table 1 can again be retitled with the following headings, Extra income (from exports), Extra consumption of domestically produced goods, and Extra consumption of imports, taking the place of *MPC* and *MPS*. A rise in exports is one way of achieving a more than proportional rise in national income. If imports rise rapidly then the multiplier effects will be muted.

(*b*) The concept of exports as an injection means that in certain circumstances it may be possible to create boom conditions by increasing exports, i.e. an export-led boom. On a more pessimistic note, however, this implies that excessive success in exports can have an inflationary effect, or that one method of checking inflation is by the leakage implied in increased imports.

(*c*) The effects of an export-led boom can be increased if, by one means or another, the consequent rise in imports can be delayed or checked. The government may contrive to isolate or partially isolate the economy from the rest of the world for some purposes by tariffs, quotas, etc. While these measures may be good for the individual economy, the effect on the world economy as a whole could be bad.

(*d*) Equally, if a government can find means of increasing exports, by subsidy of exports, or undervaluing its currency so that it undersells other countries, it may export unemployment, i.e. raise its own national income and employment level, but at the expense of worsening the problems of other nations.

Exports and imports, whether of actual physical goods or of services, constitute what is known as a nation's current balance of payments. Briefly, and oversimply, an economy which is earning more on its current balance than it is paying out is 'paying its way' : it may have economic problems but these are in general likely to be less intractable than a nation which chronically runs a deficit. It is always a lot easier – and less painful – to dispose of an embarrassing surplus than to cure a deep-rooted deficit condition.

There are, of course, other economic relationships with the outside world, apart from direct buying and selling of goods and services. Individuals or nations may decide to invest in another economy (using investment in its everyday sense), they may choose to make loans or gifts to individuals or nations, they may choose to spend money on military bases, etc., in other countries.

The effect of these economic activities cannot simply be classified as injections or leakages of purchasing power in our model. Some activities may have injection effects like exports, others may have leakage effects like imports; others, the equivalent of 'transfer' payments in the taxation element, will have little effect except, like transfers, to affect the distribution of national income and in the process affect the various marginal propensities, to save, to pay tax, to import.

The point is, however, that even if one cannot define precisely and in small compass the effects of any particular economic activities which extend beyond the boundaries of our economy, whether the model economy or the actual British economy, we can at least grasp the concept of exports and some other non-domestic transactions as injections – which conventionally can be designated X, and imports and some related activities as leakages, to be designated M.

Once again with the economy in equilibrium $X = M$. Or, putting all our injections and leakages together (again using very restricted definitions): Investment + Government expenditure + exports, etc. = Savings + taxation + imports, etc., i.e.

$$I + G + X = S + T + M$$

As before, none of the elements on the left-hand side of the equation need exactly balance the corresponding item on the other side. But in the long run in an equilibrium situation the total on one side should balance the total of the other. More realistically, perhaps, if the resources of a community are to be employed to the full then that economy has an interest in having the elements on the left-hand side, taken together, at as high a level as can be achieved without bringing about unacceptably high inflation : the right-hand side of the equation will be constantly adjusting upwards to match the level of the left.

As has been noted, it would be possible to work out a theoretical multiplier for any one of the injections in terms of propensities to save, be taxed or import, and also presumably an overall multiplier for all the injections taken together. In practice, of course, it would be very difficult to determine such a multiplier very accurately for a real economy since one simply could not verify the calculations by testing the effects of changing any or all of the elements in the equation merely to find out what happened to the economy. The only place a multiplier exists is in an economy of human beings, not a laboratory.

It is probable that in the United Kingdom the overall multiplier is relatively a low one; it is, however, very difficult to be more precise than that in a dynamic situation or even to verify the results satisfactorily within that very wide limit.

Gross Domestic and National Product

It is convenient here to introduce some more useful terminology in the language of economics and politics, namely gross domestic product and gross national product – often simply written as G.D.P. and G.N.P.

Gross domestic product is the sum total of the national economic activity for the year whether expressed in terms of expenditure, output or income. It is in a sense a general description of the output at Stage 2 of our model, i.e. it takes account only of the output within the 'closed' economy. When allowance is made for net outcome from abroad, it becomes gross national product. Both terms G.D.P. and G.N.P. will be used in later chapters.

The Principle of the Accelerator

Our main model on which subsequent discussion will turn was the multiplier, and particularly the investment multiplier. This concept permits discussion of the situation where expenditure on capital equipment tends to affect other factors, not least the level of consumption. In very general terms the point has been made that changes in the level of investment have their effects on the level of consumption.

But there is also a reverse relationship in the situation, a concept which historically predates the multiplier and which relates changes in consumption to changes in the level of investment. This is the so-called accelerator effect.

In its most elementary version the argument runs thus: suppose in the original 'closed economy without government' model there was an annual demand for 100,000 new cars, and that these were produced by 10 factories whose capital equipment had a life of 10 years before it had to be replaced. In the long run the replacement demand for capital equipment to produce the cars would amount to one factory per annum, the point about the long run being that there would be a steady annual demand of one factory per year, instead of 2 or 3 being replaced at the same time; as long as demand for cars remained steady, then so too would the demand for the necessary capital equipment in this sector.

Now let us suppose that for some reason the demand for cars changes, in this case rising by 10 per cent in one year, i.e. to 110,000 annually. On the assumption – admittedly a very big one – that the existing factories could not produce more cars, then the replacement demand for one factory would be accompanied by a new demand for one more, i.e. an increase in demand for consumer goods amounting to only 10 per cent becomes an increase of 100 per cent for capital equipment when it passes backwards along the production chain.

What would happen in the following year? Let us consider three possibilities:

(a) that growth of demand for cars continues at the same rate of an extra 10,000 cars per annum;

(b) that the demand settles down at the new level of 110,000;

(c) that the demand reverts to the original 100,000.

In the first instance, once again the demand would be for two factories – one representing replacement demand, the other representing the twelfth factory needed to produce 120,000 cars. If demand for cars increases annually by 10,000 then the demand for factories will remain at its new high level of two annually for the next few years.

If, on the other hand, the demand remains constant at the new high level of 110,000, then the demand for capital equipment in the second year drops back to the replacement demand level of one factory. Compared with the previous year demand is cut back by 50 per cent. In the long run presumably replacement demand will smooth out at 1.1 factories per year, but for the first few years demand would remain at one factory annually after a single prosperous year.

Finally if the upsurge in demand from 100,000 to 110,000 proved to have been only temporary and next year's demand reverted to the previous 100,000 cars, then the effect on the replacement industry would be even more dramatic. Since there was already one factory too many for the market the factory due for re-equipment could be allowed to go out of production, i.e. so far as the demand for capital equipment was concerned, having doubled one year, it would have sunk to zero in the next.

This phenomenon, that changes in the demand for consumer

goods can have a vastly more than proportionate effect in investment on the capital goods side, is known as the accelerator effect.
It gives some clue as to why some industries fluctuate wildly in
prosperity; it probably explains in part the as yet imperfectly
understood phenomenon of trade or production cycles.

Some Consequences of the Accelerator Principle

A point which emerges from the above discussion is that in a
modern technically orientated society, the life span of consumer
and capital goods, and hence replacement demand, does not
depend entirely or possibly even mainly on the physical durability
of goods. So far as consumer goods are concerned, their life span
often depends on convention : planned obsolescence, one of the
more dubious characteristics of a consumer society, is designed
to persuade the consumer to replace consumer goods (e.g. tele-
visions, washing machines, even furniture) by something new and
allegedly better, even if this involves the scrapping of still usable
appliances. In the case of capital equipment, decisions to replace
are probably more economically rational, depending perhaps on
technological advance, and certainly on the extent to which
replacement can be written off against taxation. A machine tool
may become obsolete within a year or remain usable for a
generation, depending on the technology of the industry. But
more often than not the replacement of a machine tool takes
place before the original has been so worn out as to be completely
unusable.

Producers of consumer durables and capital equipment constantly have to face the problem that although they would like
to see a steady replacement demand for their goods, it is only too
easy for their customers to 'make do' with equipment which
though old-fashioned or even obsolete is not unusable. Customers
in practice tend to make do in this way, i.e. postpone replacement
purchases for a few months or a year or two in times of recession
and, by so acting, change what is for them a recession into a
full-scale depression among their suppliers.

An Accelerator Effect on Stockbuilding and Stockholding

A variance on the accelerator principle can be seen in stocks held
by industry and distributors. Industry, all industry, is likely to be
carrying stocks of raw materials and fuel, semi-finished and

finished products; distributors' warehouses too will normally have adequate supplies to meet day-to-day variations in demand. Neither manufacturing nor distribution companies can run efficiently on the principle that sufficient materials will always become available daily for that day's needs, or equally that manufactured goods can be instantly converted into sales. From the point of view of the efficient use of working capital the smaller the quantity and value of stocks and work in progress the better. Computerisation and refined inventory stock control are increasingly enabling companies to avoid tying up working capital in this way. Nevertheless the fact that industry does have stocks at all stages of manufacture, though it represents a tying up of working capital, also represents room for manoeuvre by individual companies or whole industries which can have disconcerting effects elsewhere in the economy. In a period of economic uncertainty, when industry and commerce are not certain whether the next few months are going to see the onset of a recession, it is possible to delay investment decisions simply by running down stocks; equally of course when there has been a down turn in demand the corresponding down turn in economic activity may be masked for some time by the readiness of manufacturers and distributors to let stocks build up.

The difficulty that this causes is that though initially changes in stock levels iron out temporary fluctuations, they can also on occasion exaggerate fluctuations. Once manufacturers and distributors in this situation decide that stock levels have become much too high, demand will be cut back much more severely than would have been the case if the stocks had never been allowed to build up. Conversely, of course, if during a depression manufacturers and distributors have allowed stocks to run down, the subsequent turn round will be that much the more exaggerated when the economic recovery begins, for not only will they be trying to meet the increasing demand from the public but they will be trying to rebuild depleted stocks.

Variation in stock levels is not quite the accelerator principle as outlined in the earlier examples of replacement demand but its effects are much the same, i.e. to introduce an element of unstable demand. The muffling of this accelerator-type situation in stock levels is yet one more factor which makes it very difficult to predict very accurately how industries will respond not only to changes in economic activity but also to government efforts to expand or restrict output in any situation. Variation of stock-holding is as much an issue of business confidence and business psychology as rational economic behaviour, and as a result the economist may find it very difficult to predict exactly when a turning point may be reached in an economic situation in which the level of stock held is an important factor.

The Day-to-Day Functioning of the Economy

Thus far we have been considering in essence why the level of an economy changes, and whether this knowledge can be used to achieve a level of activity, e.g. at full employment, which is deemed most desirable. It was convenient to take for granted the fact that the economy will be functioning at some level or other – probably a pretty high level, even without intervention. Intervention in terms of increasing injections of purchasing power will represent only a small part of total economic activity.

In a sense a more profound question is what determines the level of activity in an economy? Obviously the injections of purchasing power, i.e. investment, most government expenditure and exports play a part; and certainly, if we want to change the level, it is easiest to do so through these injections precisely because of the multiplier effect involved.

But far more important than any of these, indeed of more weight than all of them put together, is consumer expenditure (C). In building a model of how the level of activity may change it is only too easy to neglect the point that consumer expenditure is, and in normal conditions ought to be, by far the most important factor. After all, consumer expenditure is concerned with consumer satisfaction, and consumer satisfaction is the main point of any economic activity. Investment, government expenditure, exports, all are important as components of the demand for the national product but they are of minor importance compared with the major item of consumer expenditure. Indeed they are important only in so far as they contribute expenditure and satisfaction in the future.

Consumer expenditure accounts for about half of all the national expenditure in western developed countries. It may account for more than half in poorer economies where imminent starvation or want makes it necessary to use virtually all the resources that can be mobilised merely to feed, clothe and shelter the community. On the other hand in some of the collectivist states of the communist world consumer expenditure may be less than half national expenditure because the governments of these states, in their aim for rapid economic growth, choose to put more resources into investment or other public sector use.

However even in the most growth-conscious economy with the most spartan allocation of resources to consumer needs, consumer expenditure is still likely to be the greatest single source of demand on the national product; and regardless of the standard of living or ideology of any state, consumer demand is likely to be the most stable factor, compared with the other three, namely investment, government expenditure and exports. It is the most stable in the sense that people's spending habits do not change all that quickly, unless government taxation levels (T) are drastically changed.

Later it will be necessary to examine more rigorously some of the elements of consumer demand and expenditure. But at the moment it will suffice to remind the reader that although most of this book, and indeed most government attention, is focused on the injection elements of demand already discussed, the most important activity in an economy is that which is most readily taken for granted. Ultimately all economic activity must be judged on its ability to satisfy consumer demand.

A Summary of Chapter 1

The following points have been made, although not necessarily in the order shown below.

(1) The value of goods and services produced in a country can be expressed in three ways as

   (a) national expenditure
   (b) national output
   (c) national income.

These three can be measured, with some difficulty, and since they are all different ways of expressing the same economic activity, the answer should be the same in all three cases.

(2) The main factor affecting the size of national product, known in short as G.N.P. (i.e. gross national product), is the demand for goods and services from the public, i.e. consumer expenditure. Other important items are investment (the creation

of capital goods and services), government expenditure and exports.

(3) Changes in the level, particularly of the last three, have a more than proportional effect on the size and level of G.N.P., i.e. investment, government expenditure and exports represent 'injections' of purchasing power and have a multiplier effect.

(4) Changes in the three injections of purchasing power, if left to themselves, work out of the economic system leaving a different level of G.N.P. in the process and creating an equivalent corresponding level of 'leakages' of purchasing power in the form of savings, taxation and imports.

(5) It may be possible for a government to induce changes in G.N.P. by changing any of the three injections; or to affect the operation of the multiplier effect by taking steps to alter the level of the leakages.

(6) Changes in G.N.P. brought about in this way may be in real or in money terms, i.e. the *volume* of goods and services may be changed, or their *price* may be changed, or both of these effects may be felt. The more unused resources there are in the economy – including unemployed persons – the more likely it is that G.N.P. will increase in real terms. The nearer the economy is to full use of all available resources – particularly full employment – the more likely it is that the changes will be in the value of money, i.e. inflation or deflation.

CHAPTER 2

INTRODUCING REALITY TO THE MODEL

THE previous chapter started with some unrealistic but explicit assumptions, namely a closed economy with no government. There were, however, at this stage a number of implicit, and arguably equally unrealistic, assumptions lying under the surface. They were left implicit for the sake of presenting a simplified model. If the number of qualifications which could have been made had been added at this early stage they would probably have obscured the main thread of the argument.

It is convenient, however, at this stage to backtrack and look at leisure at some of the implicit assumptions; this will be done by reference to the stage at which the assumption became important. However, before starting to examine these assumptions, these shortcomings in the argument so far, the reader should bear in mind the acid test about all of them. This is simply to consider whether the assumptions are so grossly out of touch with reality as to invalidate the model entirely. It is the contention of this chapter that even when the assumptions so far concealed are brought out into the open, the result is to muffle the economic effects discussed previously, but not to eliminate them. The economic forces described in the model become less easy to measure exactly, less easy to time exactly. But in principle they still operate. With this qualification in mind let us now look in a little more detail at the assumptions.

One of the most pervasive, and in its way most dangerous, is that because the term 'model' has been used the economy works like a machine, particularly in the sense of always producing the same reaction to the same touch on the controls. The economy is, however, not a machine. It is in the last analysis all the people in the community, and people do not react inevitably and invariably to a series of controlled reflexes.

This is a point on which it is not particularly profitable to dwell at the moment. It will, however, be a recurring theme and economists – and politicians – forget that the economy is people, at their peril.

The first assumption (on p. 9) is related to the point made above. It is simply that all activities which are economically significant are determined by purely economic motives. In practice, of course, people do not act in purely economic terms; in many significant aspects of life (even economically significant aspects), people's behaviour is not determined by economic motives : payment or reward may be irrelevant or at best a secondary motive. A vast amount of social or religious activity, for example, is inspired by non-economic motives. People do things, make things, perform services, because they want to act in a certain way or feel impelled to do so for non-economic reasons. Indeed, they may on occasion deliberately act against their own best economic interests because other motives seem more worth while.

The second major assumption (p. 10) is that in a real-life economy the information on which economic decisions are based is known accurately and instantaneously. There are very considerable practical difficulties in getting reliable information fast. To give reality to our closed economy we put figures of one million people producing £1000 million of goods and services annually. It is difficult even in the most controlled and regulated economy to be quite sure how many people there are in a country at any one time; it is even more difficult to find out how many people there are who are able and willing to do productive work. In the United Kingdom, for example, we can count the number of people who are paying national insurance – or at least we can make an estimate every three months when one quarter of the insurance cards are due to be exchanged. On the very large assumption that everyone who has a national insurance card fills it with stamps and exchanges it when he should, it would be possible to get an official estimate of the number of people who are employed or self-employed, and in the process get some idea of the type of work in which they are engaged. We can be rather faster in getting an idea of the number of people who are looking for jobs by getting a weekly count of the numbers registering for employment, or for unemployment benefits. But people have an annoying way of slipping through official checks, and most statistics are by-products of other activities yielding relevant information on the state of the economy, rather tardily and probably inaccurately.

If it is difficult in practice to establish exactly how many economically productive people there are in an economy (and the phrase 'economically productive' leaves a lot of loose ends) it is likely to be even more difficult to determine the value of work done in a year. We have given a figure of £1000 million in the model community. But it is worth considering the very practical difficulties of actually measuring this sort of value. Consider the three measures: national expenditure, national output, national income. It ought to be possible to measure each of these independently and come up with the same grand total.

National expenditure is probably the most difficult when we get down to measuring the value of consumer goods bought and sold in the course of a year. There are about a quarter of a million retail outlets in the United Kingdom, from barrow boys to hypermarkets. If any reader imagines that even with income-tax checks, surveys and censuses of all descriptions a government statistician can really trace every last penny or even every last million pounds of goods which cross the coster's barrow or the shop counter, he is being quite unrealistic. Large retail chain stores keep accurate accounts but the great mass of small shops have no very sophisticated check, and income-tax returns, supplemented by the odd census of distribution every few years, still leave a possible gap of several hundred millions of pounds which can only be guessed at.

On the savings side, it is, of course, relatively easy to obtain from banks, building societies and other financial institutions details of their deposits. But a decision merely to hold money rather than spend it is 'savings' in terms of our definition, and it is impossible to say how much money is being held for days, weeks or months, and how or why families change their habits of holding money.

National output is probably the most easy of the three to estimate, but even here the term 'easy' is relative. Not only is it important to be able to value all products as they are manufactured, but also to take account of the fact that most products use other products as components so that there is a danger of double counting if items which are produced by one firm or company reappear modified or incorporated into a product elsewhere. There is, too, a problem of valuing products whose manufacture inconveniently takes them across the end of the year for which national output is being measured, and also the problem of measuring non-material services. The present complexities in administering a new Value-Added-Tax system gives a glimpse of the practical difficulty in the far greater task of measuring all economic output annually. In general, again, tax returns can be supplemented by annual censuses but the margin of error remains large, if not quite so large in practice, as for national expenditure.

National income measurement presents problems, not merely in terms of getting accurate statements of incomes but also with respect to non-monetary incomes. So far as money incomes are concerned the main source of information is the operation of the taxation system. Taxation procedures give an indication, but not all tax returns on income, profits, etc., are all that accurate : many people simply do not pay income tax because their incomes are too small; other individuals and companies effectively avoid paying tax in the current year. There is room for dispute about what part of a person's income or a company's income really should be regarded as income and what should be regarded as necessarily incurred expense. On the non-monetary side, some incomes will have to be imputed, i.e. if someone gets certain perquisites, such as a house, the use of a company car, subsidised facilities for food, or payment in kind. For these people a summary of monetary income is not an accurate presentation.

Finally some very arbitrary distinctions may have to be made for example between a housekeeper who receives a wage and a housewife whose work in her own house is largely the same, but who is not regarded for this purpose as being in productive employment.

In all three aspects of expenditure, output and income the practising administrator is under a constraint which the theoretical economist is not. And, at the risk of repeating once again an obvious point, it is as well to remember that the information which is the raw material of economic and political decisions is not easily and accurately obtained. The point has been made that most of this information is a by-product of other activities : when it is supplemented by a direct enquiry, be it census or survey, these activities very much depend on the goodwill and co-operation of individuals and companies who can be put to a good deal of inconvenience to carry out work which is not directly relevant to their main occupation and which, frankly, brings them no particular benefits as individuals. In spite of legal sanctions which may require forms to be filled in and returned, accurate and timeous information requires goodwill from the people who have to fill in the returns. Finally, because the information takes time to collect and collate, and decisions cannot be delayed for accurate information, these decisions have often to depend upon estimates and educated guesswork.

In a wider context, if the problem of counting the population and estimating output is difficult enough in a small, unified, heavily regulated, reasonably conscientious, law-abiding, form-filling population like that of the United Kingdom, one can judge the difficulties in other parts of the world, particularly the underdeveloped regions. There no one can tell, literally perhaps to within ten millions, how many people there may be in a country. Ninety per cent or more of economic activities may be in subsistence food growing involving few, if any, money transactions. Administrative machinery of any sophistication simply does not exist, and the instinct of the population is that government enquiries mean trouble and taxation. Although virtually every nation in the world solemnly publishes estimates of population, national income, etc., in many instances the figures might diplomatically be described as impressionistic. Even in a country like the United Kingdom some of the more vital figures are at best doubtful and subject to a considerable measure of error.

Such practical difficulties can be ignored for purposes of building economic models, in the same sense that the mathematical or logical steps are unaffected by the accuracy or lack of it in the original figures. But as a matter of practical politics, the rather dubious nature of some of the estimates causes difficulties. Time and time again estimates which have gained the sanctity of printed statistics are revealed to be less than accurate long after political or economic decisions have been made on them.

The third major assumption (p. 11) is fortunately not so profound in its implications, but it does complicate real-life calculations. It is the assumption that there is a hard and fast distinction between consumer goods and services, and capital goods and services. Most products and services can be categorised fairly easily but there is a grey area where the same material or even single item can have a dual role. Thus, for example, company cars and vans can be, and often are, used in the evenings or week-ends on domestic occasions even where ostensibly they have been bought as capital goods, i.e. to help to produce other goods and services. The main problem which arises here is a variation of an earlier assumption, namely that if consumer goods can be classified as capital goods (normally therefore being allowable for tax purposes) measurement of investment based on tax figures is made more inaccurate. The problem is not too serious. But it helps to explain why it is so difficult to qualify estimates of capital or consumer goods.

The fourth assumption (p. 13) is, arguably, a derivative of one of the earlier explicit limitations. For the sake of simplicity it was assumed that stocks of goods, whether capital or consumer, work in progress, etc., became available and were subsequently used in the year of manufacture. In a real-life economy stocks may be held over from one year to another, or stocks may go to waste, so that the equation is by no means as simple or predictable as it appears.

The fact that stocks can be built up or down means that manufacturers or distributors do not respond immediately or, for that matter, entirely predictably to government measures. And when they do respond they may react very quickly, and more violently than expected precisely because of the previous delay.

The problem of the turn round is really one of confidence. Why stockholders almost overnight change their policies after a long period of inertia is imperfectly understood. But almost always it would seem that governments, when they try to stimulate or restrain output, get the timing of the turn round and the size of the effect wrong. The 'stickiness' of changes of economic activity is explicable only in terms of the size of stocks in the economy and the room for manoeuvre thus given to individual manufacturers and distributors.

The next major assumption (p. 19) is that there is a simple linear relationship between investment on the one hand and national income and employment levels on the other. In a real-life economy we cannot assume that changing the level of investment changes the other factors smoothly or proportionately. One example of the actual 'lumpiness' which develops is in terms of regional expansion. If the investment level is raised when there are different levels of unemployment in the various regions of the country, the effects are most likely to be to increase pressure in regions of full employment first. The result may be to produce over-full employment, i.e. an inflationary situation, in one region long before unemployment is cured elsewhere.

The reasons for this difficult situation are complex, but two or three stand out. First, regions of high unemployment may have obsolescent technologies and dying industries, which are just not going to survive in the long run, particularly if investment is just more of the same type of equipment which already exists in over-abundance. Secondly even if we try to concentrate spending in these regions, and make the investment of a different sort, i.e. spend in order to introduce new industries, most of the injection effects will be felt elsewhere because the equipment is likely to be manufactured in a region of newer technology. Additionally even consumer goods which mop up such increased purchasing power as is created locally will probably be brought in from elsewhere. In practice the sort of investment which does not quickly spill out into other regions is public work expenditure of the most labour-intensive sort, e.g. roadworks, etc. – hardly the ideal way of permanently introducing new techniques into a region. The unpalatable truth is that one cannot build a wall round a depressed area and stop increased purchasing power being used elsewhere. Finally, even if we have labour shortages in one part of the country and unemployment elsewhere, it is almost as difficult to move people to jobs as jobs to people. The unemployed are not going to starve in a twentieth-century economy with a welfare state. They have their roots locally, their houses, families and friends, skills and traditions which would be quite alien elsewhere. A middle-aged Tyneside miner is not going to be the answer to a shortage of sales staff in a London department store or of computer programmers in Bristol. He is not even going, very readily, to be the answer to a shortage of miners in a Kent coalfield because of the human difficulties of uprooting his family and himself which may be much greater than remaining where he is, unemployed but with a living income and with friends and neighbours with the same interests and anxieties as his own.

The last paragraph emphasises a point which is easily overlooked in a model, namely that neither investment, national income nor employment are homogeneous; nor that an application of the first always produce a given multiple of the later two. At least as profound a source of difficulty is the question of quality of investment. Investment can have spectacular results or can represent wasted effort, and a problem of the British economy is that much of its investment seems to be less effective than other countries.

The sixth major assumption (p. 22) represents gross over-simplification on the multiplier side. In the first instance the arithmetic example assumes that the marginal propensity remains constant – although obviously the developing boom or depression could affect people's decisions on how much to spend or save. Probably this assumption about a constant marginal propensity can be most seriously challenged not so much over saving as over importing, i.e. at Stage 3 of the model. A too rapid take-off in national income may produce a wavering pattern for marginal propensity to import which may climb in the first stages as distributors try to meet a sudden surge of increased purchasing power by buying overseas supplies simply because the domestic producers have been caught unawares and do not expand output fast enough.

Another more general oversimplification of the multiplier model is that each round is distinct and measurable; it would be more accurate to accept that the situation is much more confused, for the increased purchasing power will develop at different rates and at different times throughout the economy, and will soon become absorbed into other movements just as any deliberately induced ripples in a pond become absorbed into the more general motion of the water.

The next assumption (p. 31) is that governments can take effective controlled and controllable action fast. A government cannot turn public expenditure on and off like a tap : decisions to change levels of public spending can take months or even years to work through. Common sense suggests that, in a world economy like that of the United Kingdom, when the private sector is booming and using up all the resources it can command, then government spending should be held back as much as possible, whereas if the private sector is falling government expenditure should be pushed up. What very often happens, of course, is that much, most, government spending cannot be delayed and it therefore competes for resources in an inflationary manner in booms. Conversely, even in slumps, non-urgent public sector expenditure sometimes has less effect than expected, not only because the effects can take place in the wrong regions but also because these effects can be so slow and incalculable in developing that their full impact may occur only after the original situation has been completely transformed. It is not unknown for the results of changes of policy to have the opposite effect from that intended, i.e. to destabilise the situation. Cuts in public expenditure designed to take the pressure out of a potentially inflationary boom may begin to bite only after the boom has gone over the top into a slump, whose effects are then worsened; or government expenditure designed to cure a deficiency in demand can have its main impact just when inflationary pressures are beginning to show through. This is a point which has been touched upon and to which we shall have to return, but it is easy to fall into the classical error of the analogy of the economy as a machine responding in a controlled fashion to a given control. More realistically a government is rather in the situation of a doctor with an ailing patient and a supply of miracle drugs, which will probably achieve results but to which the patient's body may react after an interval which can only be guessed at, and possibly in an unforeseeable manner with all sorts of side effects which only become apparent later on.

The next assumption (p. 31) turns upon the nature of the marginal propensity to taxation. It has been pointed out that the marginal propensity to save may not remain constant, as suggested in the first multiplier example, i.e. investment. The point is even more important on the issue of taxation. The earlier *MPS* was simply an observed phenomen, i.e. a certain propensity happened to exist in a particular economy at a particular level of income. But the marginal propensity to taxation is not a given factor – it is a decision by the tax authorities on what the level of taxation is to be. In most instances taxation is progressive, i.e. in general higher levels of incomes pay more than proportionately heavy levels of taxation. It would be reasonable to assume therefore that the marginal propensity will increase as income rises, a factor which tends to dampen down the multiplier effect.

A further phenomenon which reinforces this tendency is 'fiscal drag'. Inflation has not been discussed so far, but in a modern economy where inflation is virtually endemic money incomes are likely to rise during the year and so the amount collectable in taxation rises even faster. Again this fiscal drag expresses itself in terms of marginal propensities.

A further point which has been implicitly taken for granted is that all taxation has much the same effect, particularly in this instance in affecting the multiplier. If, for a moment, we reverted to everyday language, what we are saying is that a cut in taxation will cause people to spend more, i.e. increase the effective demand in the community, and that this will happen fairly quickly. But different taxes have different effects and take different times to work through. For example, a cut in income tax which mainly benefited the lower paid would have a fairly quick result because poorer people would spend their increased disposable income virtually as quickly as it became available (and this tax cut could be passed on very quickly to weekly wage earners). This would be a 'demand rich' tax cut. On the other hand a cut in company taxation which affected the amount paid by a company in a year's time would work its way through to increased demand very much more slowly – though conceivably the effects when they were felt would be that much more profound. And, of course, in a real-life situation individual tax effects could not be isolated and identified any more than it would be possible to identify the ripples caused by a single pebble when handful after handful of pebbles of all sizes were being thrown. In the United Kingdom each annual Budget changes taxation before all the effects of last year's Budget are fully known, let alone worked out of the system.

The eighth assumption (p. 33) on the value and volume of exports and imports is a variation of an earlier one about accurate information. The fact remains that it is difficult to know precisely what is happening until several weeks have elapsed. It ought, on the surface, to be easy in an island nation to have a physical check on the value of goods entering and leaving the country. There are, as usual, practical administrative difficulties.

So far as exports are concerned, legal powers exist to insist that exporters detail the types and values of goods leaving the United Kingdom within a week or two of their actual export. In practice there are loop-holes, carelessness and inaccuracy, largely because there is generally no obvious legal or financial sanction about giving details of goods which have actually left the country. Export figures, published a few weeks after the end of the month to which they refer, are liable to be revised over the next month or two as belated information seeps in. Indeed on at least two occasions in the past few years exports have been significantly underestimated because returns were not made in full. The result was perhaps overly gloomy export figures which caused governments to take politically unpopular steps to rectify a situation. Arguably indeed some very unpopular moves and serious sterling crises could have been avoided if the accurate figures had been known. On at least one occasion the government had in a sense to make an allowance for unrecorded exports to present a more realistic picture.

The mechanics of recording exports and imports tend to work to make sure that an error presents too low figures for exports, but not for imports. The latter can be more rigorously checked when goods actually arrive in the country since customs duties may well be involved. Even here there is room for debate about the value of imports: it may be in the interest of the importer to put a value as low as possible on imports with an eye to tariff duties.

Valuation of exports and imports may if anything become more difficult to assess in the future. Any move to ease trade restrictions, e.g. Common Market membership, means that the amount of recording for permit purposes is likely to diminish and with it the flow of information about quantities and values. And increasingly with the vast expansion of the activities of multi-national corporations manufacturing products between subsidiaries in different countries, there is another dimension of difficulty. The multi-national company may, for tariff or tax purposes, put transfer prices on goods moving across national frontiers which do not correspond with the 'arm's length' price which would be charged if the buyer and seller were independent of each other.

Finally, and getting back more directly to the concept of injections or leakages, it is as well to remember that goods going overseas very often sell on credit with delayed payment and possibly instalment repayments over months or years – all of which blunt the operation of the simple model.

Some Qualifications of the Accelerator Principle (p. 37)

There are several implicit assumptions in the very simple model of the accelerator : of these three are particularly important.

The first is that factories have an exact and well-defined output. In a real-life factory it would be easy enough to establish the optimum ouput, i.e. the point at which unit costs are lowest; but it would be more difficult to define what the maximum output of the factory was. If the rising unit costs, on overtime, etc., become acceptable it may be possible to increase output well beyond an optimum or normal output. The result is that in the arithmetic example given, if the demand for cars really rose by only 10 per cent, the chances are that in the short run existing capacity would produce all or most of the new demand albeit at rising unit costs. The increase in capacity would be a good deal less dramatic and would probably take place only if there was a reasonable expectation that the increase would be sustained.

The same restraint applies one stage further back. Even if the demand for capital equipment doubled overnight (or, more strictly, over the year) the necessary capital equipment supply would not be available within the year. In part, output of existing capacity would be expanded in the same terms as with the car factories themselves, i.e. with rising unit costs; even so it is highly unlikely that the capital equipment could be brought 'on stream' from scratch within the year. Probably in a real-life situation, if it became necessary to meet increased demand very fast either at the consumer or capital goods level the reaction of prospective buyers faced with an unacceptable delay would be to import.

Finally the last of the major qualifications is that the equipment which had come to the end of its conventional life span at the end of ten years could be pressed into service to meet increased demand. Even where equipment has been entirely written off for tax purposes it is likely to be still usable. If it is not immediately sold for scrap, it may be left lying around to be used in an emergency to supplement output when demand rises unexpectedly quickly.

Notwithstanding the muffling effects which occur in real life the accelerator principle does suggest that changes in the level and pattern of consumption can have a considerably exaggerated result with unstable effects on the level of investment, and all the complications in ensuring a stable level of growth that most governments aim for.

The Role of Money

Money has several functions in the economy: the function which is most important in the present discussion is as a measure of value, of goods and services, wages, rents, profits, etc.

An important requirement of any measure is that it ought to be constant. A metre, an hour, a kilogramme are the same anywhere in the world at any time of the day. An implicit assumption in the discussion so far is that the pound sterling, which has been used in the model so far, has a constant value throughout the year or from year to year. Practical experience however suggests that any currency, the pound sterling, the dollar, or for that matter gold, have been changing value in two senses at least: (a) in relation to each other, and (b) in the quantity of goods and services they will buy. The most general situation in the post-Second-World-War era has been for virtually all national currencies to lose value over the years to a greater or less degree, i.e. any national currency is liable to inflation.

Most people are only too well aware of what inflation is, or at least does. At the moment we are sticking to the popular definition of too much money chasing too few goods.

The fact that the only practical measure of value in the model, i.e. money, is not really a constant makes it very difficult to compare one period with another. In practice it is necessary when comparing national income in one year with another to use, not the actual money values but values 'at constant prices', i.e. values that have by some means been revised to take account of the change in the value of money. At the present time, for example, British national income statistics are often presented 'at 1963 prices' to make a standard comparison possible, and it is therefore important to be sure in making comparisons whether figures are expressed in 'real' or monetary terms, or alternatively 'at 1963 prices' as opposed to 'current prices'. This qualification is easy enough to make in theoretical discussion: in practice, of course, any 'national income deflator' presents formidable problems of estimating and figures are liable to be revised from time to time.

The distinction between *real* and *money* estimates is most important in wages and salary claims based on changes in the cost of living. It is perfectly possible for money wages to rise but real wages to fall: equally it is possible for money wages to remain stationary (or even in theory fall) while real wages rise. The later situation actually happened to millions who were fortunate enough to keep their jobs in the depressed 1920s. As long as they were able to avoid having their money wages cut, their standard of living rose steadily.

Inflation, Reflation, Deflation, etc. – The Terminology of Economics and Politics

Inflation is generally speaking an unplanned, frequently an unwanted, phenomenon. Politicians and economists make conventional noises of disapproval when the subject is raised: in practice, however, most governments find it convenient to have a little inflation, say 2 or 3 per cent annually. It is an almost painless way of repudiating past loans and obligations without too much overt discredit. Particularly, it seems, because the main sufferers, the small holders of government securities, national savings, etc., are not economically sophisticated enough to appreciate what is happening to the value of their holdings. In fact the powers that be in any economy really start worrying about inflation when it gets to the stage where the general public starts reacting to the situation in such a way that the whole monetary system is threatened; the industrial and commercial sectors of the economy are sophisticated enough to look after their own interests when inflation is small-scale but endemic. They worry only when the rate of inflation threatens to get out of hand, or more subtly when the rate of inflation varies unpredictably from year to year. One can work out the cost of borrowing or lending when there is no inflation or steady inflation; violent fluctuations in the rate cause more problems.

Although inflation is generally unplanned there is a planned activity which has rather similar results. This is *reflation*, which may be defined loosely as pumping more purchasing power into the economy to stimulate demand and so increase output in a period of recession. For most of the post-war period, the implication that this was to some extent a respectable version of inflation could be ignored, on the grounds that most of the rise in output which resulted was in real terms, i.e. more goods were produced, rather than prices being raised. Presumably, however, the nearer one got to that low level of unemployment where a real rise in national income shaded off into a monetary rise the more difficult it would become to claim that reflation was not inflation. Thus in the late 1960s and early 1970s, when it proved possible to have inflation coexisting with heavy unemployment and unused resources, there was perhaps something odd about talking of reflation while simultaneously complaining about inflation. A justification can be made, which depends on the identification of different kinds of inflation – and this will be discussed later. But however intellectually convenient it may be to distinguish the effects of inflation from those of reflation common sense suggests that the distinction in some cases is more in the theory than in the practical results.

The other point about inflation which has been made is that it redistributes national income: some sectors gain, others lose.

Curative action to halt the rise of inflation or to check expansion getting out of hand is called *deflation*. This may be achieved by cutting investment or taking other steps to put the multiplier effect in reserve, or by making it more difficult and more expensive to borrow to expand output. It will raise the value of money, if pushed hard enough, will create unemployment and will redistribute national income, but to different sectors of the community than those who benefit from inflation.

Deflation used to be, and in some quarters still is, a dirty word because it was associated with the massive unemployment of much of the inter-war years. For a few years after the Second World War, when this revulsion against the concept was at its height, the curious term *disinflation* was invented, and it was alleged that this was somehow different. The term 'disinflation' has tended to fall out of use. It was in many respects a gloss for a policy which was probably necessary for the national good but which was just as unpleasant for the individual whose job was threatened. Curing inflation is almost inevitably an unpleasant experience for someone.

Money and Real Income

One of the most obvious implications of the changing value of money is the effect this has on individual incomes, e.g. in the form of wages. Rises in the cost of living, whatever that some-what vague phrase may mean, are a very potent argument in demands for wage increases: the demands that are in turn countered by the claim that wage increases are themselves inflationary. Both elements in this circular argument are, of course, valid, but at the same time the individual wage-earner gets more immediate benefit and his trade union representative more prestige out of an increase in money wages, even if everyone knows that the effects are going to be inflationary and against the interests of the community as a whole.

Annual wage demands are now so much an ingrained part of industrial affairs that it is hard to remember that little more than a generation ago the situation was completely different. Sustained inflation and annual wage claims are a very recent phenomenon, and the two are intimately inter-related.

The same phenomenon also applies to other types of income. The fact that the annual rent of a ninety-year-old house may be as much as the total original cost of building illustrates this fact graphically.

Inflation in the United Kingdom has not been so great or so long sustained as to develop its own logic and set of rules. But there is no doubt that a persistence of the situation of the early 1970s would ensure that new rules would emerge as they have emerged in other parts of the world where 20 per cent inflation has been experienced for years.

Interest rates, for example, on loans can climb to rates which would seem fantastic, but in a situation with a built-in inflation in double figures make sense. Even in the United Kingdom when inflation has on occasion been at a 10 per cent annual rate, people have effectively been borrowing at a zero or even negative rate of interest because the interest rate has fallen to or even below the level of the rate of inflation.

These curious situations are illustrations of the fact that there can be a very marked difference between real wages, rents, interest, etc., and their current monetary equivalents.

It will be necessary to look at the implications of changes in the value of money and the causes and cure of inflation in more detail and with a good deal more precision later on. But for the moment the following points are worth considering, some of which have been spelt out, and some of which have not.

(1) The fact that money changes value makes direct comparison between one time period and another difficult.

(2) Inflation is not simply a rising tide, to use a popular cliché, affecting all prices and all individuals impartially. Some prices rise faster than others, some sections of the community can get their money incomes to rise faster than others, faster indeed than the rate of inflation. The really important social and political fact is not merely that inflation raises prices but that it redistributes national income. Some sectors of the community do very well out of inflation, others suffer correspondingly.

(3) Inflation tends, when left alone, to cure itself, but only if governments are prepared to accept the distribution of national income involved. Most governments are not, and as well as trying to cure inflation, possibly by deflation, they may try to redistribute income back the way it was before inflation took hold. This deliberate redistribution can be socially just, even imperative, but is a diabolically difficult problem administratively and politically and to a large extent any success the government has may prolong the inflationary process by frustrating the self-curing mechanism.

(4) Notwithstanding (3) inflation is an international phenomenon – nations export and import inflation and it is difficult to isolate an economy from inflationary or deflationary pressures elsewhere. The only way to tackle inflation may be on a world basis.

(5) Finally there is some evidence that even fairly severe inflation can be tolerable, once the community learns to adjust its commercial practices to the situation. But a rate of inflation which fluctuates from year to year adds a new dimension of uncertainty which is at least as damaging as the inflation itself.

CHAPTER 3

COMPARING THE MODEL WITH REAL LIFE

THUS far, the model has been expressed in fairly abstract terms. The final chapter in this section will attempt an interpretation of the economic situation in the United Kingdom in terms of the model. Three periods of contrasting conditions will be examined:

(1) A decade in the inter-war years, from about 1925 to 1934
(2) A post-war decade, 1955 to 1964
(3) The situation from 1966 to 1970

In each case a brief factual summary will be followed by a somewhat loose analysis in terms of the model

$$I + G + X = S + T + M$$

(1) *The Inter-War Years from 1925 to 1934*

It may be argued that this period is beyond the personal recall of the great majority of potential readers, indeed is now firmly embedded in history rather than economic theory. This is, however, unfortunately, only partly true, for the realities of this period, particularly unemployment, and indeed the myths of the period, still exercise a baleful influence on U.K. economic and political thinking.

Briefly the late 1920s was a period of deflation, high unemployment and industrial stagnation in Britain, although for most of the period the rest of the western world was enjoying relative prosperity, compared with what had preceded it and what was to come. The reason for Britain being the odd man out was the determination of the British government to restore the international standing of the pound sterling which had been damaged gravely by the First World War. In pre-1914 days the pound had been literally as good as gold; as a result of the war Britain had left the gold standard and the value of sterling had fallen. Most major currencies had done even worse but relative to its chief rival in international finance, namely the dollar, sterling had suffered badly. In an attempt to restore its pre-war eminence as the international currency, the British government tried to force up the purchasing power of sterling by a policy which included raising interest rates, i.e. making for 'dear' money and in general restraining demand. The policy appeared to have succeeded by the beginning of our period in 1925 when a modified gold standard was restored. But the result for the remainder of the 1920s was that the new gold value of sterling was too high in relation to other major currencies. British export prices were too high, import prices were relatively low. The British traditional interest in free trade, on which nineteenth-century prosperity had been based, hampered the introduction of substantial tariffs, with unfortunate effects on employment.

As long as the remainder of the western world remained prosperous, the situation, though difficult, was not intolerable. The world situation, however, began to change in 1929 when the American boom burst. By 1931 the U.S. depression had become a world-wide depression. The British government, after six years of struggle, had to give up its attempt to maintain the gold standard and the value of sterling sank. The necessity for deflation and dear money to protect an overvalued currency had gone. Unfortunately the United Kingdom was as vulnerable as anyone else to the world-wide slump. The British economy suffered less than, for example, Germany or the United States in the 1930s but because it had started off from a lower point.

By the middle 1930s, with unemployment standing at around three million, the situation of depression had all the signs of permanency and the general belief among economists that unemployment on a massive scale was a transient condition was shaken. The new analysis, the General Theory evolved by Keynes, emerged but remained a somewhat heretical doctrine for some time. What began the recovery ironically was the imminence of the Second World War and the drive to rearm. Even so, at the beginning of the war in 1939 unemployment was still over one million.

Analysis in terms of the Model. What was happening to the various injections of purchasing power, namely investment, government expenditure and exports, an increase in any of which, according to the model, ought to have had multiplier effects?

In a period of deflation and dear money there was little incentive to invest. Borrowing was relatively expensive, and since the value of money was rising in real terms, the cost of repayment would be greater than the value of the original loan. Confidence, a fragile concept, was never strong, and even when deflation ended in 1931 slump conditions made the outlook appear even more gloomy.

Government expenditure was likewise falling. In times of financial stringency there was an economy drive on the public sector. This idea of rigid economy made sense so far as any individual was concerned, but when pursued by a central goverment it made the situation worse. It is difficult to estimate the value of G, i.e. public expenditure as defined earlier, but in the late 1920s and early 1930s it was probably around 12 per cent compared with about 30 per cent a generation later.

Some government spending on public works to relieve unemployment was eventually tried. But even here there was confusion of aims and a tendency to economise when a little public extravagance would have made more sense. Even the United States, where the famed New Deal saw public-works expenditure rise, the effects were psychological rather than real because the administration tended instinctively to go for the most 'economic' policies. Indeed, by a supreme irony Nazi Germany, with its massive, indeed grandiose, programme of roadbuilding and rearmament, had gone further to solve its economic problems, in pursuance of its military and political ambitions, than did the liberal democracies, unwillingly approaching the reality of rearmament.

Exports too made little contribution to increasing the national product in the United Kingdom. In the early days overvaluation of sterling, in the later period world slump and growing tariff barriers, frustrated any multiplier effect.

On the other side of the equation, a high level of savings by people fearful of losing their jobs and high imports stimulated by the conditions which hit exports represented large leakages. Only relatively low taxation (neutralised by a balanced budget) represented the small leakage which a large multiplier required. Indeed arguably the multiplier was working in reverse as every cut in investment, government expenditure, and exports produced more than proportionate effects.

Apart from the injection elements, the main component of demand was consumer expenditure. Here there was little incentive to spend with the imminent prospect of losing one's job.

With hindsight it would have probably been far better to have gone in for massive public expenditure, based on deficit budgeting, i.e. borrowing. There was certainly a vast backlog of public sector expenditure which would have made Britain a happier and healthier place; and if the policy of raising the value of sterling had not had first priority, exports too could have been pushed up. At the worst, if the dream of restored free trade had been abandoned earlier, tariffs might have played their part in reducing the leakage. Instead Britain had a decade of economic stagnation, mass unemployment and a legacy of industrial bitterness which is still a potent factor in the political climate today.

Hindsight is, of course, only too easy. But the intention of this retrospective review is to suggest that even the comparatively crude and simple model of the economy, in terms of injections and leakages, can be used to explain what went wrong and what could have been done to remedy some of the worst ills of the period.

(2) *A Post-War Decade, 1955 to 1964*

Like the first decade this is rather arbitrarily chosen in this instance to cover a period when the immediate effects of the Second World War had worn off, and when the United Kingdom was moving into what has become known, as a term of abuse or sarcasm, as the affluent society. The phrase had a bitter taste for many but certainly when compared with the inter-war decade it was a period when, to use a misquotation of the time, 'You've never had it so good'.

It was a period of reasonable growth, full employment and some inflation. The statistics give the general picture. Between the beginning of the decade and the end, average annual growth in the economy was nearly 3 per cent. Comparable figures for the inter-war decade are not available because the national product figures for the earlier period were not collected in a comparable form, but it is doubtful whether growth was much more than a third to a half at most of the post-war figure. Unemployment during the same period averaged about 1.8 per cent – about

375,000, a fraction of the inter-war figure. Inflation averaged rather under 3 per cent annually, compared with a deflation of about 2 per cent in the inter-war period.

The lesson of the inter-war years had been thoroughly learnt. The prevailing problems were over-full employment with inflation always a present possibility, not the mass unemployment of the inter-war years.

There were a number of unsatisfactory aspects to the situation. This was the notorious period of 'stop–go', i.e. successive credit squeezes followed by fairly rapid expansion. The problem was that rapid expansion created, not so much inflation, as balance-of-payments problems. These caused crises of varying degrees of severity in 1955, 1957, 1961 and 1964.

It would not be strictly true to say that priorities had been completely reversed. The continuation of a strong pound sterling was a priority aim for the British government, which was committed to the maintenance of sterling as an international currency. But although it was a priority it was not the dominant priority of the inter-war wars. In other words the major priority was full employment. But whenever the policy threatened to create excessive inflationary pressures, particularly in the form of a balance-of-payments crisis (i.e. when significant numbers of sterling holders began to fear that the currency would be devalued, then priorities were reversed, with a credit squeeze and dearer money to strengthen the international position of sterling, at the temporary expense of stopping and pushing up unemployment.

The political crises of the period, in particular the Anglo-French invasion of Suez in 1956, had remarkably little effect on the economic situation. In the long run it was the continuing weakness of sterling which caused most difficulty.

In hindsight the major crises were those of 1957, 1961 and 1964, not only because they were progressively more severe, but because they provoked government reactions, which broke the self-imposed restraints of earlier crises. As it happened, the measures had mixed success, but they did foreshadow the time when most of the preconditions which had been established in the post-war years were to be swept away in the 1970s.

The significant factor about the 1957 crisis was that for the first time in the post-war period very severe credit restrictions were imposed by use of interest rates. Bank Rate was up to a

C

post-war high of 7 per cent. Such a rate was reckoned at the time to induce high unemployment and therefore was regarded as political suicide. As it happened, it was not. The Conservatives won an election two years later on an increased majority. The real damage was economic rather than political, in that it paved the way for even more severe restrictions the next time round, with unfortunate effects for business morale. In that sense the government bought more freedom of action, but at the price of laying industry more open than before to unpredictable credit squeezes, disastrous both to morale and long-term investment plans.

The 1961 crisis was in its way as dramatic and depressing in its implications, in particular because the Chancellor, then Selwyn Lloyd, attempted with limited success to introduce a wages and prices freeze, without, however, being able to impose it successfully. It was the ultimate lack of success rather than the freeze which probably cost votes.

The early stage of the 1964 crisis was marked by a dramatic and, as it turned out, unsuccessful change of strategy. When the sterling reserves began to fall – the harbinger of yet another crisis – the new Chancellor, Mr Maudling, tried a new tack. Instead of imposing a credit squeeze in the early stage, he held fast to a policy of rapid expansion in the hope that the evidence of rapid growth in the economy would fend off the crisis of confidence, which lay behind the crisis of sterling.

A cynic might say that the Conservatives, in a period of political unpopularity and facing an imminent election, had little choice but to carry on with expansion, at an unprecedented post-war rate of nearly 6 per cent for the year. As it happened the crisis was still very much there and was effectively used by the Opposition in the election campaign. In hindsight what proved disastrous for the policy was the unwillingness of the government to follow its own logic. If growth were to be given first priority then sterling should have been permitted to depreciate. As it happened, expansion and an overvalued pound sterling could not be sustained simultaneously in 1964.

The Conservatives went out of office on an expanding economy but a disastrous external deficit, and the new Labour government soon applied conventional methods of restoring the external situation, in the process cutting growth at home.

Analysis. Leaving aside for a moment the first injection considered, i.e. investment, let us consider the development of the other two, namely G (public expenditure) and X (exports and similar activities).

So far as public expenditure was concerned this was a period when there was no shortage of projects on which public sector spending could be and was justified. In the inter-war decade discussed, public expenditure in our definition was about 12 per cent of the national total. During this second decade it was about double this and rising fairly steadily. An important factor in this was expenditure on armaments at the height of the Cold War. Public expenditure of about one quarter of the national total goes far to explain the constant pressure of demand, added to marginally by the rise in transfer expenditure which probably accounted for another sixth of the total.

If public expenditure was high, exports persistently failed to match up to hopes or expectations and, as we have seen, a sterling crisis was always potentially just over the horizon. It was, of course, this fact which helped to explain why inflation grew as slowly as it did. The persistent trade deficit with its accompanying high imports tended to mop up inflationary pressures and the frequent recourse to credit squeezes helped to contain inflation albeit at the expense of steady and sustained growth. Eventually the implication of persistent balance-of-payments crises was that sterling was overvalued, as it had been in the 1920s, and in time devaluation proved to be inevitable – although not till after the close of the decade under question.

The whole problem of exports, exchange rates and inflation illustrated the practical constraints which existed for any government. If sterling crises were to be avoided, then exports had to rise much faster than imports. But had they done so the inflationary situation would have become that much more difficult since the multiplier effect would be felt against a background of full employment. Even if, on the other hand, the government had been willing to pay the political price of devaluation (which it was not, because its own prestige and the future of the sterling area system was at stake), then devaluation might have proved a temporary remedy to the balance-of-payments crisis but would have been a further boost in inflation.

The economy staggered on – sometimes growing fast, sometimes fitfully. If inflationary pressures could have been reduced then there might have been a chance of faster growth without the 'stop–go' situation. But how to reduce the pressure? Public expenditure remained obstinately high, rising overall during the decade; cutting exports would have made economic nonsense and so as often as not the cuts on the injection side had to be borne by private investment – the very item on which so much future growth and prosperity would depend. The problem so far as private industry was concerned was that it was impossible to plan for sustained investment or growth, because almost certainly the next credit squeeze was only a year or two away. In some ways the psychological damage to confidence was as great as the economic consequences of 'stop–go', and the unwillingness of the private sector to invest in expansion when the times were economically propitious probably arose from the well-founded scepticism engendered among industrialists.

The problem was that the multiplier effect was too great. Could anything be done on the leakage side to take some of the pressure out of the system? National savings were, of course, encouraged, and responded reasonably well, perhaps in the long run too well, for when a few years later the government would have liked to have seen consumption rise, savings obstinately stayed up. Taxation could be and was used in the form of surplus budgeting to mop up purchasing power; the trouble here was that with taxation at a relatively high level there was less incentive to work harder for more money. Lastly imports were a source of embarrassment, not a viable means of decreasing the pressure.

Many of the instruments of control discussed earlier were being perfected during this period, and it was also at this time that the difficulties of getting as near as possible to full employment without overbalancing into inflation were arising. What did emerge from this period fairly clearly was that the government was rather effective at bringing down the level of demand, if it were prepared to be ruthless enough. There was, however, a certain amount of trouble being stored up for the future. It appeared that there was a national buoyancy in the economic situation. No matter how severe the measures which were taken to deal with a crisis by way of a credit squeeze, as soon as the restrictions were eased the economy would rapidly revert to a state of increasing pressure of demand and full employment. To use an overworked

cliché of the period, it appeared that taking one's foot off the
brake was equivalent to putting one's foot on the accelerator
pedal. During this decade this was a reasonable assumption;
later on this condition changed and in the 1970s, as it happened,
there were emerging two separate problems : (*a*) when to brake;
(*b*) when to accelerate. There were times when a future government was apparently to try both simultaneously.

(3) 1966–70 – The New Combination, Inflation and Unemployment

It might seem somewhat arbitrary to pick the year 1966 as the
beginning of a new phase. After all, a new Labour government
had come to power in 1964, committed to ending the 'stop–go'
cycle, and at the same time inheriting a serious and prolonged
sterling crisis. For that matter 1966 did not even mark the end
of that crisis, which rolled on until the end of 1967 when a
three-year battle to save sterling from devaluation failed.

Nevertheless 1966 was significant. It marked a revival of the
crisis and the abandonment of the heady promises of a new
approach enunciated at the time of the 1964 election. As it
happened, the scale and severity of the steps taken were to be
felt for several years ahead – indeed well into the 1970s.

The credit squeeze of 1966 appears in hindsight to have produced a change in direction of growth, and unemployment –
and the devaluation which eventually came produced, or at least
contributed to, a new burst of inflation. Between 1966 and
1970 the rate of growth fell to 2 per cent – indeed after an exceptional rise of 3.5 per cent in 1968, a false dawn, it showed every
sign of a fall which was to last for four years; unemployment rose
slowly but steadily past the low average of the past two decades
and in 1970 was standing at 2.5 per cent; and inflation rose to
an annual figure of around 5 per cent. In fairness to the government, the situation was to accelerate when the Conservatives
came into power in 1970, but the latter were entitled to argue
that they had inherited the situation, just as in 1964 the Labour
government was entitled to blame their predecessors for their
initial difficulties.

Chronologically the pattern between 1966 and 1970 was as
follows : the sterling crisis which had smouldered on for two years
burst out again, and was met in the traditional manner – a very

orthodox credit squeeze and more massive borrowing overseas and from the International Monetary Fund to stave off a run on sterling. It was only to be expected that the immediate effect on output and employment would be severe but possibly, on the evidence of past crises, temporary. However this time, as the pressure eased off, unemployment did not fall; instead it began to move upward slightly – the beginning of an accelerating trend which was to go on for years. The figures for national output, when they became available a few months later, also heralded a slowing down in growth which persisted over the next few years. The change was not clear at the time – the delay in pick-up might have been a temporary lag; in the event however the failure of output to recover was probably the first occasion in the post-war era when it was becoming apparent that taking the brakes off the economy might not be enough to produce accelerated growth.

As it happened however the main attention was focused on the immediate crisis issue, namely the threat to the sterling exchange rate. The run on sterling was halted by the sheer volume of international aid and loans which were poured in to hold sterling's exchange rate. But the underlying crisis – and arguably the crisis was an overvaluation of sterling – persisted until a forced devaluation came about at the end of 1967.

In a limited economic sense of remedying an acute currency crisis, the 1967 one was undoubtedly successful – after a heart-stopping delay. In political terms, however, it was botched, and arguably the internal economic measures which were introduced to ensure its success made the consequences costly and long-lasting. The previous Chancellor had resigned and the new Chancellor, Mr Jenkins, apparently determined, once and for all, to bring the persistent weakness of sterling to an end, imposed restraints on internal demand on a very heavy scale. In six years of office the Labour government raised taxes very substantially, much of this rise being part of the post-devaluation measures. In the 1968 Budget, for example, the rise in taxation was about £900 million – forced saving on a very heavy scale. Although this heavy taxation increase was in part balanced by a steady increase in public expenditure, the net effect of successive tax increases was probably an 'overkill'.

The errors of the Labour government were probably com-

pounded by the failure of the Conservatives in 1970 to realise
that the overkill had taken place. This, however, will be discussed
at a later stage in the book.

Analysis. The most significant development of this period, more
significant, perhaps, than the spectacular collapse of a twenty-
year policy of maintaining the sterling exchange rate, was the
emergence – tentatively at first, but with increasing clarity – of
a new combination : inflation and unemployment on an unprecedented scale. It had been assumed on the basis of more than
twenty years of post-war full employment, with inflation barely
contained, that unemployment or inflation were equally alternative, not complementary, evils. What had gone wrong?

One possibility is, of course, that the analysis in very simplified
Keynesian terms outlined in the first chapter as injections and
leakages of purchasing power either never had been, or no longer
was, valid. Certainly the phenomenon of inflation and unemployment was a unique one, and one which on the face of it appeared
to be quite incompatible with the model. With a number of
qualifications about the events which led up to the situation in the
late 1960s it is still possible, after a fashion, to reconcile the
model with reality; the reader may be left to judge whether the
model is still plausible.

The most important qualification is one already alluded to,
namely the danger of assuming that the economy operates like
a machine. The particular danger of this analogy lies on the
timing and the degree of reaction to a change in circumstances;
what is clear is that an economy is not likely to react in exactly
the same way every time a certain action is taken. Society, or
more strictly in this instance the body economic, is rather analogous to a living body. The analogy is almost as dangerous as the
machine analogy; society, short of a catastrophe, is for all intents
and purposes immortal. Nevertheless it does exhibit the biological
characteristics of growth and decay, though it can alternate these
in a way a body cannot. If, however, we accept the broad analogy
that in many important respects society is a living body – and
after all what is an economy but the people living within it – then
the Keynesian remedies of injections or leakages can be likened
to modern miracle drugs. They have quite decisively banished
the illness of the inter-war years, but like miracle drugs they are
beginning to show the drawbacks.

First, remedies as efficacious as these can have side effects which are not always understood, or indeed apparent for some time. Thus it could be argued that each crisis and the credit squeeze which proved so effective in curing the immediate problem went far to destroy the morale and confidence of the private sector of industry, to the extent that the buoyancy which had been apparent in the system disappeared in time. By the middle 1960s, after credit squeezes almost every two years since the end of the war, industry simply did not believe it would be allowed to invest or expand capacity without yet more credit squeezes – particularly as the expected beneficial effects of devaluation took so long to show up.

Secondly, pursuing the biological analogy, bodies build up resistance even to miracle drugs; if the latter are used frequently then the dosage has to be increased every time. More concretely this suggests that if it becomes necessary to remedy a chronic situation such as inflation or a balance-of-payments crisis year after year, more and more drastic measures may have to be taken. Certainly the evidence was that each crisis was more difficult to control than the last and required more drastic measures, and borrowing from overseas to cope. In the case of the 1967 devaluation the crisis really began over three years earlier, and even a year and a half after the devaluation deflation was still a dominant theme. In this sort of situation it is hardly surprising that business confidence was at rock bottom by the time devaluation could officially be said to be working. Confidence and expectations are not mechanical or quantifiable factors, but they play a vital role in deciding how and if the economy will react to government policy.

The latter factor is complicated by the problem of a time lag which inevitably occurs between a change in policy and its effects. It has already been suggested that it is very difficult to estimate what the time lag will be in any particular instance. Some policies will have almost immediate effects. A change in pension rates for the retired will almost certainly have an impact on the economy very quickly, for the average pensioner has such a modest standard of living that he or she will spend most of any increase on necessities. In economic jargon the marginal propensity to consume of pensioners, like any other poorly off group, is very high. Other tax cuts, however, will take longer to take effect and the effects are a good less easy to anticipate. Thus a cut in company taxation or a change in the system of investment allowances works much more slowly for three reasons: (*a*) they cannot for very valid administrative reasons be introduced quickly; (*b*) the individual company is likely to mull over the new situation in the light of the general feeling about the situation; (*c*) even if the firms do react as the government wishes, the effect, i.e. an increase or decrease in capital investment, will not have its full impact overnight.

There is in fact substantial empirical evidence to suggest that major decisions on tax changes take eighteen months or more to have their full effects. Thus one can have the slightly unnerving situation that, with annual Budgets, the changes which are obviously taking place in an economy may not be the result of the last Budget, but of the one before that.

The result of this delay, and the uncertainty as to when in the medium-term future the effects will be felt, can have a serious effect on policy in a democratic society. The public at large are just not ready to believe that changes take as long to work through as they do and as the delay before a hoped-for change in the situation takes effect, there will be public and parliamentary pressure to do something, anything indeed, to improve the situation. To do nothing at all may in some respects be the policy which requires the most courage. Putting the problem at its most cynical, if the appearance of action becomes a political necessity, the problem may be to drum up a programme which sounds impressive but will have relatively little effect. If 'too little and too late' is a standard cliché, too much and too often is at least as big a problem. It is quite probable in hindsight – and everything is clear in hindsight – that too much was done in the late 1960s and the overkill effect on the economy lasted for years.

Finally, we must consider specifically the extent to which the injections/leakage approach can be reconciled with the simultaneous growth of inflation and unemployment (though to be just to the Labour government, the worst effects took place in the early years of the incoming Conservative government).

The first point is that the persistence of inflation was a political rather than a purely economic phenomenon. Persistent inflation generally is not allowed to run its course and cure itself, in the process redistributing national income. Governments, and particularly Labour governments, have very clear ideas on how they wish to allocate national income and by resisting the redistribution they may do much to perpetuate the inflationary situation.

The second point is the obvious one that devaluation is an inflationary remedy unless the government is able to stop incomes rising. To quote Mr Wilson's notorious *gaffe*, the pound in your pocket was devalued and most people realised that. The fact that once devaluation was a *fait accompli* virtually everyone said that it ought to have been done sooner has given rise to an unfortunate feeling that devaluation is somehow a painless technical device with no side effects; its side effects on prices were profound, particularly as the government conspicuously failed to hold down wage and salary settlements and its income policy collapsed.

The third point about inflation at this time is that it was a world-wide phenomenon. In a very open economy like the United Kingdom it was hard to avoid the consequences, particularly of the Americans' huge and persistent balance-of-payments deficits, which were probably creating a situation where inflation in the United States, as a result of the Vietnam war, was being contained by passing its effects on to other areas, particularly western Europe.

So far as unemployment is concerned it is at least arguable that the failures of the economic model to match reality in the late 1960s was due to political failures, not economic theories going wrong. People do not starve even if they are not particularly mobile and able or willing to move to where vacancies exist. In a welfare state system the average unemployed person does not even have to accept any vacancy which comes along, but can in practice refuse what he regards as unsuitable jobs for a long time before any sanctions are brought to bear. Allied to this is the fact that trade union strength, or at least the unwillingness of governments and managements to challenge them if this can be avoided, means that it is quite possible for trade unions, even in a period of unemployment, to force up members' money wages. Indeed the smaller the skilled labour force relative to the capital investment in capital-intensive industries, the more incentive there is for the employer to buy a temporary peace by meeting wage demands, if he can pass them on or if they are a small proportion of his operating cost.

In the last analysis it is probably attitude as much as economics which determines wage structures. British management in general has been reluctant to face up to aggressive trade union bargainers; after nearly three decades of labour shortages, and the surrender of the Labour government to trade union pressure in dropping its industrial relations legislation and statutory incomes policy in the late 1960s confirmed the relative strength, which had passed, possibly by default of leadership elsewhere, to the trade unions.

PART II

OBJECTIVES AND PRIORITIES IN THE ECONOMY

Thus far we have looked at the mechanics of an economic system, more particularly the British economic system. Now we may profitably consider the use to which the economic system may be put. This is not exactly a question which seems to spring to the mind of the general public or the politician – the answer seems a common-sense one, but it is well worth considering this very fundamental issue and the implications, particularly the need to reconcile different and possibly conflicting objectives.

An obvious and valid objective might be summed up as consumer satisfaction. This might seem a remarkably materialistic summing up of a system but, in its broader sense, consumer satisfaction is the aim of any valid political and economic system; not necessarily of course in the mere quantity of consumer goods but in all the material and spiritual values which might be summed up, with deliberate vagueness, as the good life. Materialistic or mystic, every individual is concerned in this sense with consumer satisfaction. There is obviously a wide difference of interpretation about what this ought to be, but in a western economy, indeed in most economies whatever their ideology, a substantial measure of material comfort is high on the list of priorities. Economic considerations and therefore economic objectives may be only one facet, but they represent a vital aspect of any society, and it is with economic objectives, tempered of course by non-economic considerations like ideas of equality, that we are primarily concerned in this book.

There are at least five which can readily be identified; these are listed below, but without any attempt to list in order of priority :

(*a*) rapid economic growth,
(*b*) full employment,

   (*c*) a fair share-out of national income,

   (*d*) a reasonable economic balance among regions,

   (*e*) reasonably constant prices.

These objectives will be considered individually in more detail but there are a few points which can be noted immediately. Hitherto we have assumed that (*a*) and (*b*) were the same thing, i.e. the way to rapid growth was through full employment. In a very general sense this is true but in the specific situation which governments face from day to day, rapid growth and full employment are not necessarily the same thing.

The implication of this has a general application, namely that all these objectives are not necessarily compatible; indeed they may be completely incompatible on occasion, and the job of the politician is to decide on the priorities. Moreover the priorities change; and again it is basically the politicians' job to decide when to reshuffle priorities.

Another point, which again is essentially political – or even moral – is that the objectives are shot through with phrases like 'reasonable' and 'fair' which cannot be objectively quantified. The stuff of policies is to decide what is reasonable and what is fair.

CHAPTER 4

RAPID ECONOMIC GROWTH

THE problem of obtaining faster growth in the British economy is one of the most important facing any government. The unpalatable facts are that the rate of growth of the British economy has been, since the Second World War, and very probably for most of the twentieth century, far less than most industrial nations of comparable technology.

One result of this has been that the very substantial lead which Britain had in its standard of living, relative to other industrial nations, has been steadily eroded. In the early 1950s after the major war damage to European industry had been repaired, Britain had probably the highest standard of living of any European country except possibly Sweden. By the early 1970s, using the same sort of measures, Britain had a lower standard of living than every country but one north of the Alps and west of the Pyrenees. The one exception was Ireland whose economy is a virtual annex of Britain's.

This decline had happened not because the British standard of living had fallen. Manifestly the great majority of British people were enjoying more affluence than in the 1950s, and moreover had seen the economy expanded at a greater rate than in any other two decades of her history. But while the British economy grew at a historically fast rate for twenty years, virtually every other country in western Europe grew far faster, so that G.D.P. per head – the measure used so far – in all these countries rose to the point that in the 1960s most countries of comparable industry were registering a higher G.D.P.

The reasons for this relative lag in the British economy are clearly very complex, and frankly ill understood. Some of the issues will be discussed in more detail. But one of the reasons why the British government decided on seeking membership of the European Economic Community, the Common Market, appears to have been the hope that in some way or other the factors which had produced such a rapid growth rate among the original six members of the Community would rub off on to Britain if she became a member.

While this increasingly urgent thrust for growth has been developing it is ironical that there has been a somewhat para-doxical movement in parts of the world, particularly in the developed and therefore affluent societies, decrying the doctrine of 'blind growth' for its own sake. There are, to be fair, arguments for limiting growth, some sound, some superficial, few economically convincing and virtually none politically acceptable to the non-affluent majority of the electorate of any democratic society.

The arguments which probably carry most weight are based on an extrapolation of existing trends. These suggest that if world demand for raw materials – oil is one of the most fre-quently quoted – continues to expand at the present explosive rate, then world supplies will be exhausted in the foreseeable future. Some raw materials may indeed run out before the end of the century. A variant of this theme is that the developed nations are using up the world's resources at a rate twenty or thirty times as fast as the underdeveloped parts of the world and that the increasing affluence of the former is being won not only at the expense of future generations, but at the expense of the majority of people alive today, in the underdeveloped areas.

The arguments cannot be discussed let alone refuted in detail in the present context, but an important point in mitigation can be made about future development. Most prophecies of doom appear to assume no technological progress; on that basis most economic activities can be convincingly demonstrated to result in famine or disaster by extrapolation of existing trends far enough; in the past similar prophecies of doom have been overtaken by technological advance aided by the price mechanism which ensures that whenever a chronic shortage of one material or product appears likely, the steady rise in price calls forth an acceptable replacement

The second part of the argument that the developed countries are using up more than their fair share of existing resources is more difficult to refute on economic or technological grounds because it is a moral rather than an economic argument. But the whole issue of rapidly rising populations and inadequate resources is likely to come to a head in the supply of food, long before it does on the issue of raw materials in general.

Many of the arguments against rapid growth represent very long-term considerations. Unfortunately perhaps the anti-pollution lobby has become a rather fashionable preoccupation; like most fashions, much of the current concern may be replaced by something else in a few years' time, with the real kernel of truth dispensed with along with the husk. At the moment there are sections of the community which urge different priorities and acceptance of a slower rate of growth, if this is the price of seeking more desirable objectives. But at the risk of being accused of cynicism one can only observe that the rejection of material values rarely comes from the worst-off sections of society, for example pensioners, whose judgement about whether affluence has gone far enough might be rather more soundly based.

The overwhelming argument for faster growth is that it lessens the insoluble dilemma of distributing the rewards of an economic system. The distribution of the national income is at least as much a political or moral as an economic argument, and is the subject of continuous and often bitter debate in a democratic society. But when a hungry (or greedy) family is squabbling over sharing out the national cake it makes life easier for the harried mother to have as large a cake as possible; and there is little doubt that extra growth and then extra national wealth make most political as well as economic problems easier to solve. To argue that somehow Britain's rate of growth is really a pattern for the future, for the whole western world, is to evade the problems of the shortcomings in the British economy. If, in the future, Britain and the West in general choose to settle for slower growth than at present, then it ought to be precisely that, namely *choice* not necessity.

Productive Capacity and its Utilisation

There are two aspects to the problem of determining the rate of growth in an economy. The first of these is the physical and technological one, namely what are the factors of production, particularly in capital equipment and skilled labour which are available : the second, an economic aspect, is how to ensure that the available resources are used to the best advantage, and added to at the most appropriate rate. The physical and technological aspect is comprised under the heading of *productive capacity*. The economic aspect can broadly be described as the *management of demand*, i.e. how to ensure that the purchasing power within the community is just right to keep a constant pressure of demand neither underutilising nor overworking the available productive factors.

Productive capacity will be discussed in this chapter; *demand management*, one of the key political and economic problems of any British government, is the main theme of the third section of the book.

Productive capacity then might be defined as the capital equipment, technology, skills and manpower available to produce. In any developed country it is likely to grow steadily, and, incidentally, change in content with capital equipment, technological know-how and intellectual skills growing relatively faster than manual skills or the demand for unskilled or semi-skilled labour.

The Growth of Productive Capacity

It is, of course, impossible to measure exactly the productive capacity of an economy, since this is not merely a matter of physical output, but of output in one sector of the economy traded off against forgone output elsewhere, and numerous other factors, only some of which are economic. Nevertheless in very rough-and-ready terms the available evidence suggests that productive capacity has been growing at over 3 per cent per annum in the two decades between 1950 and 1970. Before 1950 figures are not particularly relevant against the background of the wartime stresses on the economy. From 1970 onwards there were some hopeful signs that capacity might be rising faster but it is on this twenty years that solid evidence is available.

Before looking at the methods of assessing growth, one very elementary method of looking at the overall trend is to graph the figures of national output between 1950 and 1970. The picture is of overall growth with peaks representing boom conditions. These peaks in fact have a strong negative correlation, after a time lag, with unemployment figures; this is a somewhat involved way of saying that when output was at its peak, unemployment was heading towards its lowest, and that the latter series followed the opposite direction to output, but a few months late.

As output rose or fell, unemployment after a delay fell or rose.

Common sense suggests that the peaks of output represented the maximum use of productive capacity. If the same information is graphed at constant prices (i.e. the effects of inflation are eliminated) then the peaks of output ought to give an indication of how productive capacity is changing. Of course, it is impossible to join the peaks with a straight line but an approximate line gives the gradient of 3 to 3.5 per cent growth, with possibly evidence of a rise at the latter end, possibly towards 4 per cent.

On the (very large) assumption that productive capacity was growing at a fairly constant rate during this period it is apparent that actual output was generally below the maximum, and that this phenomenon was particularly noticeable during the late 1960s (the possible reasons for this have been discussed in the last chapter).

The situation can be illustrated by considering changes in G.D.P. in percentage terms (Table 2).

TABLE 2

Year	Real G.D.P. Percentage change	Year	Percentage change
1950	3·2	1961	2·6
1951	3·0	1962	1·2
1952	0·2	1963	3·8
1953	4·0	1964	5·7
1954	4·0	1965	2·9
1955	3·7	1966	1·8
1956	1·2	1967	1·6
1957	4·2	1968	3·6
1958	0·2	1969	2·0
1959	4·0	1970	1·7
1960	5·7	1971	0·9
		1972	3·5

It is important to realise that actual output is not the same as productive capacity and that in at least half of the years shown output was growing at less than the productive capacity. In several years of course output was rising faster than productive capacity as calculated earlier, which would suggest that the economy was moving towards full output and mopping up unused capacity inherited from earlier years.

It seems logical to assume that when productive capacity puts a limit on the rate of growth one can expect growth in output over the level of growth in productive capacity only if there is unused capacity from past underutilisation. But the converse relationship may be more important. If there are several years of slow growth, then productive capacity may well move downwards on to a lower path, because industry is not likely to go on and on investing in new capital equipment if the present resources are year after year being substantially underutilised. In passing, the reader may care to consider why the new Conservative government of 1970 found that it took more than two years of exhortation and tax cutting to persuade a demoralised private sector that in spite of its years of underused capacity, it ought to plan to invest in yet more capital equipment.

In other words it is important that

(a) productivity capacity be used as near the limit as can be achieved, the limit being set by production bottlenecks and/or inflation;

(b) the limit be pushed up beyond the historical 3 to 3.5 per cent possibly to the 6 or 7 per cent comparable nations achieved in this period.

Both the gradient (i.e. the rate of rise of productive capacity) and the gap between actual and possible output (the concern of demand management) matter; and although they are being considered separately they are inextricably interwoven.

Alternative Methods of Measuring Productive Capacity

The method of projecting the line joining the peak capacity points in the economy is, of course, a very crude method of assessing productive capacity. There are three methods which give a rather more logically based measure, which can at least supplement the figure given by extrapolation.

(a) It may be possible to find out from individual companies the amount of slack they have, measuring this as the extent to which they are operating below their capacity. When the individual results are collated however it soon becomes obvious that there are difficulties in aggregating the result. In most factories there is not a clearly defined physical limit; indeed long before the output lines seize up with overloading, diminishing returns and soaring costs impose more practical restraints. Moreover it can often happen that potential capacity consists of obsolete or obsolescent equipment which can be pressed into service in an emergency, or when profit margins are high enough; the potential spare capacity is not really comparable with existing capacity, and most factories operate perhaps 10, 20 or 30 per cent below what could be physically produced – indeed they are intended normally to do so. If the average capacity utilisation of factories works out at about 80 per cent this is very far from saying that national productive capacity is being used only at an 80 per cent level. If every company which had spare capacity began to step up output simultaneously and speedily, shortages of key labour or materials would almost certainly materialise in the form of rocketing costs long before anything like full capacity on a national scale was in sight.

In passing, however, it is worth noting that this qualification of rapid expansion is important but in one sense a temporary phenomenon. Bottlenecks are rarely absolute in a technologically dynamic economy and over time they tend to be overcome if growth can be achieved at a steady rate rather than a spectacular burst which invites a bottleneck. All bottlenecks disappear in time.

(b) A second measure of spare capacity is the amount of unemployment existing. This measure is however by no means a satisfactory one and its validity has become more suspect over the period since the middle 1960s. Between the end of 1965 and the end of 1971, the numbers in civil employment (including self-employed) in Great Britain fell from about 24.9 millions to 23.6 millions, i.e. by well over one million. At the same time, output measured by G.D.P. rose by about 12 per cent, measured in real terms.

In part these apparently contradictory trends can be reconciled in terms of rising productivity per person employed: by the end of this six-year period productivity was rising at about 5 per cent. Nevertheless in the context of measuring spare capacity the information about unemployment leaves something to be desired.

The problems of measuring and dealing with unemployment will be discussed in more detail in Chapter 5. Suffice it to say at the moment that there are at least two important factors at work. Neither employment nor unemployment is a homogeneous quantity, i.e. there may be unused manpower resources available during a period of shortage, but of the wrong skills and in the wrong places. Secondly, the numbers of registered unemployed do not necessarily correspond with the numbers actually unemployed, nor is there a constant relationship between the registered and actual numbers. Not the least puzzling aspect of the 1966–71 figures is that while jobs were disappearing, unemployment was rising much more slowly : fast enough in all conscience but at a rate equivalent only to about half the jobs being lost. Even allowing for the point made above about registration, the situation is by no means fully understood. But though the issue will have to be examined in more detail later the main point to be noted is that involuntary unemployment represents unused productive capacity in its most poignant form; it is clearly not an entirely reliable indication of overall unused productive capacity.

(c) A third measure, like the second, expresses productive capacity in terms of human resources but in the form of unfilled vacancies. This has a fairly clear link with capacity in the sense that a fall in the number of vacancies notified presumably indicates increased use of resources. A variation of this might be to look at the ratio of numbers registered as unemployed to the number of registered job vacancies.

The criticisms which can be made of registered unemployment can by and large be made about registered vacancies. Nevertheless, taken by itself the figures for vacancies are a fairly good guide to the situation, provided they can be broken down by industry and region.

Finally, in dealing with any measure which depends on figures of people employed or unemployed, the point has been made before – and will be made again – that statistics of numbers are by-products of other activities, rather than being directly and continuously compiled by actual counting for that purpose. It would be comforting to believe that even in a highly regulated society like the United Kingdom it is possible to identify precisely the numbers employed, their ages, skills, incomes, etc., or even the numbers who are really looking for jobs. Realistically however we must accept the fact the information available is, frankly, patchy.

The Utilisation of Productive Capacity

The reader may well feel that the distinction between the growth in productive capacity and the actual growth rate is somewhat confusing. It is worth repeating therefore the point that productive capacity sets the limit on the rate of growth, but that the rate of growth in the long term affects productive capacity, particularly in a situation where more and more excess capacity results from slow growth. It is the objective of demand management to try to match up growth rate to productive capacity, both because unused capacity represents wasted opportunity and because if unused capacity grows substantially investment in productive capacity is cut back.

One of the big problems in the British economy in the late 1960s and 1970 was that actual demand and output had not matched up to the growth in productive capacity. Between 1966 and 1971 G.D.P. had expanded by about 12 per cent, capacity by possibly 20 per cent. This was hardly a healthy situation if growth in productive capacity was to be maintained at 3 to 3.5 per cent, let alone expanded.

Arguably in a free enterprise society it could be left to market forces to bring about the right pressure of demand to ensure that productive resources were used to the full. But in a mixed economy, and most western economies are of this type, the size of public sector demand, which is determined by government policy, is likely to play a dominant role, being responsible for about a third of all demand. If the government is not willing or able to take on the role of controlling demand, it has at least to intervene fairly actively to influence the rate of demand, to reduce it if it appears to be growing faster than productive capacity, for so long as production bottlenecks or inflation appear; or alternatively to stimulate demand if it is falling below productive capacity.

This is an issue which will be discussed in detail later, but two points can be made now. First, that so far government interventions to control demand have been rather hit-or-miss affairs with considerable dangers of mis-timing or overkill effects taking place. And it is clear that a government can check excessive growth far more readily than it can stimulate growth. An appropriate analogy might be that of a doctor, who does not really cure a disease, but if he treats the patient correctly produces conditions for the body to recover by its own recuperative powers, while if he diagnoses badly he may worsen the condition.

It has been seriously argued that demand management in the terms so far discussed has done little to help growth in the British economy, and in fact may on occasion have worsened the difficulties, by mistimed or inappropriate measures. It is difficult however to see how governments can avoid playing a decisive role if public sector claims on the national resources are going to continue on anything like the present scale. And all the indications are that the public sector will, if anything, expand, almost regardless of the political complexion or desires of the government.

International Differences in Productive Capacity and Growth Rates

The reasons why any particular country should have a slow or fast rate of growth in productive capacity is frankly baffling.

One explanation which has enjoyed considerable popularity is the so-called technological gap, the argument that countries with the most advanced technologies, like the United States, can achieve faster growth than the more backward countries. This might explain why a relatively primitive economy in Africa or Asia might find it difficult to become an advanced industrial society, but it scarcely explains why a country like Britain has a lower growth rate than countries of a comparable technology, for example Germany, or even more strikingly Japan, whose growth rate throughout most of the post-war period has been explosive, far exceeding that of the United States.

Even where technology is not available in the most up-to-date form, it can be bought or licensed, and there is no reason to assume that this is a general situation explaining British performance. If anything British technological achievement is in many respects ahead of its European competitors, though British industry often seems unable to turn that fact to its advantage.

A second argument is market size, and there is probably some substance to this. The technological options open to industry increase with the size of the market. Very large production plant ought in technical terms to be able to produce at lower unit cost than small plants and the size of the plant is directly related to the size of the market. The bigger the market, the bigger the plant; the more specialisation within the production unit, the more and cheaper the unit cost in mass production. This is one reason why, for example, membership of the Common Market, which has brought so much benefit for individual industries in some of the founder members, like Germany, France or Italy, seemed so desirable to the British government in the 1960s. But although, as has been said, there is some substance to the argument, relatively small economies outside the major trading blocs, like Sweden or Switzerland, do very well. Market size is a factor which matters, but which can be circumvented.

A more plausible explanation is in terms of relative rates of investment. In the early 1970s it was known that the proportion of G.N.P. which went to investment in the United Kingdom had been rising, rather patchily, over the past decade. Nevertheless it was still only about 18 per cent compared with an average of about 23 per cent among the original Common Market members and 35 per cent in Japan. The real problem, however, goes deeper than the levels of investment in two respects. Although the differences in level of investment correspond roughly with the levels of productive capacity, this still does not explain why British industry invested at such a relatively low level in spite of generous tax and other financial incentives. The second, lesser, difficulty is contained in the phrase 'correspond roughly': there is some evidence that the quality as well as the quantity of investment leaves something to be desired.

There is, of course, no single solution, and there are possibly elements of truth in the three arguments listed above. But possibly the most relevant factor is the least qualifiable, namely that curious self-fulfilling factor, already touched upon earlier, of expectations. The argument that British industry has relatively low expectations of growth is that after two decades of growth, fast enough in historical terms, but constantly restrained from taking off spectacularly by repeated external financial crises and credit squeezes, British industry was conditioned into the situation where low expectations of rapid growth in consumer demand for its products led to low investment; subsequent slow growth confirmed the expectations, so that even after the original very real constraint was officially downgraded, if not dropped in the early 1970s, the conditioned reflex had been established. A good illustration of the frustrations inherent in this situation was the situation facing the new Conservative government in 1970. After several years of slow growth, it could with some confidence expect that output would now expand steadily. Since the average growth rate over the previous four or five years had been well below the rise in productive capacity, and there was no pressing balance-of-payments problem, the pattern was set for growth. Even if the new Conservative government did not cut taxation to increase demand, the outgoing Labour government estimated growth could be expected at about 3 per cent annually. In fact, in the first year of the Conservative government growth was virtually nil and the government then spent about a further year frantically stimulating consumer demand by cutting taxes and credit controls, and extolling the opportunities now opening up for industry in the Common Market. In the event, it proved difficult enough to get consumer spending to rise and very difficult to stop investment actually falling. What seems to have happened was that industry simply refused to believe that after twenty years of 'stop–go', they had a government which would not cut back in investment in the event of another crisis. The problem was, of course, that if reluctance to invest lasted long enough, the period of slow growth which industry feared would come about, and so justify their fears.

If this hypothesis is indeed correct, then the encouraging element in the situation was that if expectations could be reversed by a few years of rapid growth it could be hoped that a new conditioned reflex of high expectations leading to high investment and fulfilment of these expectations might be established, i.e. a virtuous circle instead of a vicious one. Whether the necessary years of growth could be sustained was, of course, the vital issue.

The Standard of Living

At the beginning of this chapter the overall objective of government policy was defined as consumer satisfaction, in the widest sense. If growth in any economy is to be more than an international status symbol, then it has to be converted into some more meaningful measure, i.e. a standard of living.

The idea of a standard of living is relatively easy to grasp but very difficult to quantify. As a starting-off point it may be useful to consider the G.N.P. expressed per head of the population of several countries in order to get some idea of relative standards of living.

TABLE 3

Changes in the standard of living measured by G.N.P. per head at 1963 prices and exchange rates[1]				Percentage change Annual rates	
	1960	1965	1970	1965/1960	1970/1965
U.K.	1502	1708	1865	3·4	2·2
U.S.A.	2937	3460	3845	4·8	3·2
France	1546	1924	2447	5·8	5·8
Germany	1531	1838	2243	5·0	4·6
Japan	533	817	1372	10·0	12·1

Source: O.E.C.D.

An obvious point which emerges from Table 3 is that the G.N.P. figures do not in practice make it very easy to compare the standard of living of one country with another. Most people would accept that the United States has a higher standard of living than the United Kingdom, and this is borne out by the G.N.P. figures. This is not however quite the same as saying that the United States has a standard of living twice as high until we know rather more about the cost of living and general ambience of the society.

The situation is rather more complex when one compares France or Germany with the United Kingdom. According to these figures the standard of living in France was higher than that of Germany. In 1970 the gap had grown since 1960, and incidentally both were higher than for the United Kingdom. As at least a subjective judgement, a number of people with experience of all these countries might find it difficult to accept the comparisons. It would in these cases be difficult to avoid bringing in a discussion of the cost of living in the countries and how this had changed over the years – which is why it has been necessary to quote at fixed prices. In part too the reader might suspect that

[1] Figures for 1971 onwards are difficult to establish because of the floating exchange rates which then became a feature of the international scene.

although all figures had to be converted into dollars the exchange rate value of the currencies, particularly in the light of the devaluations and revaluations which have been omitted, was open to question. This is perfectly true : unfortunately however if we take account of changes in exchange rates we would have to assume that, for example, the British standard of living fell by 14 per cent in November 1967 – a proposition that is manifestly absurd, in spite of the Prime Minister's unfortunate assertion 'The pound in your pocket has not been devalued'. It had, but not overnight by 14 per cent.

The example of Japan has been included not only because of the spectacular rise in G.N.P. of that country, but to emphasise the very considerable difficulty in comparing a standard of living in the Japanese context with that of a western country.

If it is difficult to compare the standard of living of one country with another, it is presumably easier to compare changes in a country over the years. The figures given on the right hand of the table illustrate graphically how the rise in G.N.P. in the United Kingdom has lagged behind that of other countries, at a reasonably compararable state of development.

Having said this one may push the argument further and ask whether changes in the G.N.P. per head are quite the same as changes in the standard of living. The answer, unfortunately for the aim of putting a measure on this, is that the relationship between them is probably not too accurate. The main reason is that a variable amount of G.N.P. will be appropriated for public-sector spending and then used in ways which can hardly be said to add to the standard of living. At one extreme, expenditure on the armed services may well be vital to a nation's survival, but not many citizens would feel that an increase in the number of tanks or aircraft available to the armed forces represented a rise in the standard of living.

There are however other types of public-sector spending whose effects might be difficult to measure, but which could not be dismissed out of hand as having no effect on the standard of living, for example expenditure on the health service or public education. Not all the community uses these services all the time, but if the effect of government expenditure is to make these services available free of charge or at a reduced cost to individuals, it would probably be widely agreed that this type of expenditure did raise the standard of living of the community, not least by taking away the burden of anxiety of an individual who feared crippling medical costs if he or his family became ill.

Other types of public expenditure which arguably improve the overall standard of living might be schemes to improve the environment, by demolishing unsightly buildings, shifting debris, building roads, improving public amenities; the difficulty with such expenditure is to put an annual money value on improved amenities, particularly per head of the population.

Thus so far as our actual quantitative measure of changes in the standard of living is concerned, it becomes necessary to exclude this real but unquantifiable aspect. What remains is G.N.P. per head less the cost, in terms of taxation, of all government expenditure, i.e. real disposable income, that income left to the individual when all direct taxation has been levied. Table 4 shows the gradual rise in real disposable income per head of the population over ten years, in money and percentage terms. In view of changes in the value of money and in population size during the period the figures are only approximate, but probably reasonably reliable. For purposes of comparison the equivalent G.D.P. percentage rise is also given.

TABLE 4

DISPOSABLE INCOME (1963 PRICES)

	£	Per cent increase on previous year	G.D.P. increase on previous year
1963	407	3·9	3·8
1964	421	3·4	5·7
1965	428	1·8	2·9
1966	435	1·6	1·8
1967	440	1·1	1·6
1968	446	1·5	3·6
1969	447	0·2	2·0
1970	462	3·3	1·7
1971	473	2·3	0·9
1972	492	6·6	3·5

The comparison with G.D.P. figures is the most interesting. It suggests that though there is a relationship between a rise in national output and rise in the standard of living in the new, very narrow, measure of real disposable income it is not directly proportional.

The most obvious reason for fluctuations is probably the level of taxation : by implication raising the level of taxation reduces the standard of living – an obvious point perhaps until we accept that the taxation may be improving the standard of living in the non-quantifiable areas discussed earlier. If the increased revenue is used to improve the environment, the 'quality of life', to use a question-begging phrase, or to give a higher income or better amenities to the pensioner or the less well-off, we are back into areas of value judgement which cannot be quantified, but are no less significant for all that.

Another factor which may cause the real disposable income to vary its relationship with G.D.P. is change in the price levels. The point of 'real' prices, in this case revaluing at 1963 prices, is to try to eliminate this bias, but it can only do so in very general terms particularly in respect of consumer prices.

Lastly, but by no means least, in a country like the United Kingdom which depends so much on trade with the rest of the world, disposable income is likely to be affected by movements in the terms of trade : this latter concept can be defined roughly as the ratio of the prices we have to pay for imports compared with what we get for exports. The most obvious example is in the price of raw materials which are liable to fluctuate wildly from year to year for reasons which have little to do with events within the United Kingdom. It is quite possible to envisage a situation where output is rising, G.N.P. in real terms is increasing, but because of movements in the terms of trade, real disposable income falls : or alternatively a mediocre performance in the home economy with little or no growth can still produce a situation of a rising standard of living because of relatively falling import prices.

Lastly, the concept of real disposable income as a measure of the standard of living takes no account of changes in the pattern of leisure. In some of the most unpleasant or dangerous jobs in the economy, coal mining for example, absenteeism may be as much as 20 per cent on occasion, i.e. a miner may choose to work a four-day week instead of increasing his income. Whether this decision represents in any meaningful sense a lowering in his standard of living is very debatable.

In the long run the main determinant of the standard of living, whether measured to include non-quantifiable benefits or in the very narrow but measurable terms of real disposable income per head, is the rate of growth of G.D.P. But to talk in absolute terms of changes in the standard of living from one year to another is difficult : comparisons between countries are even more difficult. Economists or politicians can make general assertions about how the standard of living is rising. But to pretend to measure the rise in very precise terms, is asking for trouble.

The Trade Off: More Goods or More Leisure

Western man seems to have an almost infinite capacity to consume more and more goods and services. But even this apparent insatiability masks important changes, a move in many instances away from physical consumption to other objectives. High on the list comes the pursuit of leisure; some of the complications of this have already been alluded to in connection with the problem of measuring the standard of living.

Sometimes the decision to opt for leisure is an overt one. Demands for shorter working weeks and longer holidays are obvious examples. Where a claim for shorter working hours is a demand which means exactly that, the issue is clear and the economic costs can be clearly assessed. Unfortunately there may also be instances of concealed decisions to opt for leisure whose results are more difficult to assess. A glaring example of such concealed leisure was to be found in some British industries in the 1950s and 1960s where the pattern was simultaneous over-manning and regular overtime – a combination on the face of it as unlikely at the time as substantial inflation and unemployment.

The situation can be traced back to the wartime and immediate post-war experience of a chronic shortage of labour. Trade unions, fastening on the short-term interests of their members, fought tenaciously not only for higher wages but for shorter hours, resisting redundancy even where jobs became physically less exacting as the capital equipment to back up labour increased. Weak management in some instances, fearful of losing scarce labour and aware that increased costs could often be passed on to the customer, offered little resistance, their surrender being conveniently covered by government-appointed arbitrators whose policy more often than not was to split the difference between the so-called 'final offer' of employers and 'minimum demand' of the union.

Per se high wages and short hours are no bad thing for an economy in the long run. Higher and higher wage costs are the best incentive to technological innovation and the most efficient use of resources, as American industry has convincingly demonstrated. But there was an unfortunate twist to the British situation – or more accurately three twists :

(*a*) Increased wages were not matched by increased productivity during most of the period.

(*b*) Shorter hours were not worked to the extent that the official work week was cut; what happened in many instances was that nearly the same hours of work were put in but overtime rates were paid at an earlier stage. Worse still there was every incentive to spin out work as long as possible so as to make overtime a regular feature of the work.

(*c*) Even where improved methods of production were introduced there was very strong resistance to moves to cut labour; management remained obsessed by memories of chronic labour shortages of the past.

The essentially fragile edifice of underproduction and overmanning began to crack in the late 1960s. The process was accelerated in 1970 by a new government which, unlike previous Labour or Conservative governments, was not initially excessively concerned to conciliate the trade unions. An acute credit crisis and the sudden awareness, after years of rising unemployment, that manpower shortages were a thing of the past, seems to have produced a new realism among employers. The unemployment rate soared for the first time in a generation to over a million, without a corresponding fall in output. British industry was, belatedly and for a time at least, becoming more productive, and a quite exceptional rise in productivity followed.

There are several morals which can be drawn from this, but the one with which we are concerned here is the question of what the developments meant in terms of leisure.

Shorter hours worked represent more leisure. But so arguably do longer hours spun out unnecessarily. Management and workers who choose to work below a comfortable capacity are opting for a form of leisure too. The manager who arrives an hour or two later than his continental counterpart, who enjoys a two-hour business lunch, might deny the charge indignantly. So too might the worker in an underworking and overmanned shop floor. But if one examines the rise in productivity per head in the early 1970s and the embarrassingly high level of unemployment this produced it is difficult to avoid the conclusion that the *malaise* described on the continent as the English sickness, or by an American observer as half-time Britain, was perhaps a rather masochistic method for a community to opt for more leisure rather than more goods.

CHAPTER 5

FULL EMPLOYMENT

THERE are two good reasons for making full employment an aim for any government:

(*a*) the fact that unemployment represents waste of resources in its most acute form,

(*b*) the political and psychological effects of unemployment.

It is only too easy to assume that these two reasons are the same, or that they are at least always compatible. Unfortunately on occasion they are not. It may make economic sense to tolerate a degree of unemployment, even a high degree of unemployment, particularly in a society which is undergoing rapid technological change. In this situation attempts to cure unemployment by retaining jobs may slow down and distort changes which in the long run are going to benefit the community as a whole. But the effects on individuals of, in effect, being thrown on the scrap heap in the prime of productive life can be heart-breaking. Society may on occasion regard it as being legitimate to delay change to prevent such a situation arising for too many people. Either the economic or the social course may be chosen; after all society is not committed to pursue solely economic ends. What is perhaps less excusable is the situation where a social decision is taken at the expense of economic efficiency, and then the issues are blurred either deliberately by political expediency or because of intellectual laziness so that the results are presented as not only socially, but also economically, the best course. Lame ducks may be worthy of some sympathy on occasion; but they are still lame ducks at the end of the day, not swans.

The concept of full employment. Full employment clearly does not mean that everyone who wants to work has the job he wants, where he wants, all the time; such a situation, even if it were possible, would imply immobility and therefore stagnation. There is always likely to be a pool of workers, at the very least changing jobs and taking several days or weeks to make the change; also in all probability movement from one job to another will be slowed down by the fact that people who are leaving or being shaken out of their previous jobs may have inappropriate skills, training, or even attitudes to new employment. There cannot always be an easy switch from one type of job to another. Nor are people perfectly mobile.

The normal situation therefore is that there will be a number of unemployed seeking suitable jobs and a number, conceivably a greater number, of unfilled vacancies being notified to employment offices. A rough-and-ready rule might be that full employment existed in practice when the number of unemployed and the number of registered vacancies were about the same, even though for the reasons mentioned the two sets of problems represented by the figures could not be married up.

It would make more economic sense in many instances to use unfilled vacancies as a measure of the use of resources. Registered unemployed, however, is the concept which makes most impact on the general public and on the politician, expressed as the percentage rate of unemployment.

The most widely quoted percentage is probably the 3 per cent unemployment mentioned in the Beveridge Report on Social Security published in 1942, which became the cornerstone of the post-war social security system. Compared with the 8, 9 or even 10 per cent unemployment which had been only too common in the 1930s, 3 per cent unemployment, as a definition of attainable full employment, did sound at the time an almost unrealistic dream. In fact in the post-war years for about two decades 3 per cent was regarded as unduly high; 1 or 2 per cent was the politically acceptable normal. Empirical results, as has been noted, suggested that very low percentages represented the danger points of inflationary pressures. Demand management was used in the 1950s and 1960s to aim for these figures, in so far as they could be achieved without inflation or too frequent balance-of-payments difficulties.

One of the insidious dangers of the very praiseworthy effort to ward off high unemployment was that overfull employment rather than excess unemployment was the norm. As we have seen, the fact of chronic labour shortages, or more strictly the threat of labour shortages, made employers exceedingly unwilling to shed surplus labour. Rather they would carry excessive labour on their wages bill and endeavour to pass on the cost of overemployment

to their customers. This employers in general did with considerable success, at least in the home market. They were less successful
at passing on the excess costs in overseas markets where competition was stiffer.

The situation of excessive labour in many industries continued
at least into the middle 1960s with consequent overmanning,
resistance to change and resistance to labour saving. For reasons
discussed in the last chapter there was a quite startling change of
attitude in the middle 1960s which, however excellent for the
long-term prospects of British industry, proved to be an immediate
source of embarrassment to the Labour government and even
more to its Conservative successor in 1970. When employers
found their profit margins being seriously eroded they began
seriously to attempt to recoup at the expense of wages bills and
unemployment soared.

The dilemma of the government was acute. It could scarcely
but be happy at the sudden rise in productivity. The most obvious
political issue however was rising figures on unemployment. The
situation was understandable, if hardly agreeable, during a
recession, such as that which followed the credit squeeze of 1966.
But it was embarrassing for the government to find that even
when it was able to stimulate growth in the economy again by
1972, unemployment remained obstinately high even though
output was rising at a record figure. By the early 1970s there
was therefore a good deal less emphasis, at least on the part of
government, on the concept of full employment and a good deal
more on the desirability of rapid growth. So far as unemployment
was concerned, though it was being spelt out that a million unemployed was an unacceptably high figure, it was virtually impossible
to get an authoritative statement about what the acceptable level
of unemployment would be.

A minor point which may be made about the figures in
Table 5 is that because they are monthly averages for each year's
figures, they are in practice seasonally adjusted. This is not perhaps too important in the present context. Virtually anyone who
has ever looked at figures such as employment or unemployment
figures will be aware that some occupations are very seasonal,
and the fact therefore that unemployment figures rise fairly
rapidly during the winter months does not automatically indicate
a rapidly approaching depression. Nor does the fact that employ-

ment rises again in the spring automatically mean that boom
conditions are on the way.

TABLE 5

EMPLOYED AND REGISTERED UNEMPLOYED, GREAT BRITAIN 1963–72
(000s)

	Total employed[1]	Registered unemployed[2]	Percentage
1963	25,138	520·6	2·3
1964	25,268	372·2	1·6
1965	25,463	317·0	1·4
1966	25,583	330·9	1·4
1967	25,391	521·0	2·2
1968	25,233	549·4	2·4
1969	25,207	543·8	2·4
1970	25,044	582·2	2·5
1971	24,827	758·4	3·3
1972	24,782	844·1	3·7

There is, however, one important political issue here. News-
paper reports of monthly changes in employment or unemployment tend to concentrate on the more obvious changes, i.e. the
seasonally unadjusted figures, and the results can be to show
emotively bad or good results over two or three months, whereas
what really matters is the overall trend once the seasonal factors
are removed.

Very many economic series are now produced on a seasonal
basis; in some instances, indeed, the government departments do
not even publish the true figures (i.e. with the seasonal element
still shown). Presumably in the case of the politically very
emotive figures on employment the department concerned
publishes both the seasonally corrected and the uncorrected

[1] A minor problem about figures of employed or unemployed is that
definitions may vary according to the way in which figures are collected,
and a certain element of redefinition may take place on occasion from year
to year. In the present example the figures for the employed relate to June
of each year, and show a gradual but steady fall after a peak in 1966.

[2] The numbers of registered unemployed represent the average for each
year.

figures, hoping, usually vainly, that the commentators will pay more attention to the seasonally corrected figures. They are no doubt justified in claiming that the corrected figures are the ones that really matter; unfortunately the corrections which are made are based on historical data, and there is always a danger that seasonally adjusted figures will fail to show up long-term changes for some months, turning points in the economy thereby being obscured. And the fact that the seasonal adjustments are from time to time redefined may mean that a praiseworthy attempt at accuracy is seen as a political move to 'cook' figures.

Table 5 shows the intriguing fact already mentioned that numbers of people who appear to lose their jobs do not show up subsequently in the unemployment figures. This is probably politically a bonus to a government in a situation of falling job opportunities. The empirical evidence suggests that over the past few years for every two or three people who lost their jobs only one subsequently showed up in the unemployment register; it is by no means clear, however, that there is a constant ratio between the number of people losing their jobs and the numbers officially appearing as unemployed.

It must be admitted that there is no absolutely watertight explanation of the phenomenon of the disappearing unemployed. What is clear, however, is that it is naive, even dangerous, to assume that the published figures tell the whole truth, either on employment or even more on unemployment.

The practical difficulties arise in part from the point frequently made, that information of this nature is a by-product of other administrative processes.

So far as employment is concerned there is, of course, a legal requirement for employers to make available to the authorities the numbers of their employees, not only for social security, but also for tax purposes. Ignoring the fact that small family concerns, particularly shops, may be somewhat vague on the subject of who in the family is employed and how he or she is reimbursed, there is still a very practical administrative problem. Even where information is available, and there are no irregularities in defining who is or is not employed, the fact that the information is available if collected does not mean that it will or can be collected instantaneously. It may be several months before the number of people in employment in a particular week will be known reasonably accurately; absolutely accurate figures may take so long to arrive that the information is of historical interest only, because decisions affecting employment just cannot wait. Up-to-date information, i.e. not more than a week or two out of date, may depend on sample surveys and an element of educated guess-work.

In practice of course the politically sensitive issue is not the number of people in employment but the number out of employment; and if it is difficult, even in the face of legal sanctions, to get accurate figures of people in employment, it is infinitely more difficult to find out who is unemployed. There is no legal requirement to register as unemployed, and in looking at the figures it is important to consider the motives for registering.

Why do people register as unemployed? The obvious answer, and almost certainly the main answer, for most people is that they want work. A second answer, which is not quite the same as the first, is that they are claiming unemployment benefit and related social-security benefits; or at the least getting their insurance cards franked so that they are not liable to pay their weekly social-security contribution.

However, when an individual goes along to an employment office and registers this does not mean that he is willing to accept any job. Certainly, in determining whether a person is available for a job and willing to take it, the Department of Employment officer does not assume that any job will do for any applicant. But, as might be expected, the willingness of an individual to opt for a period of unemployment, provided comparatively generous social-security benefits are being paid, varies. Not all that much is known about the motivation of people who become unemployed, if for no other reason than that the unemployed are no more a homogeneous mass of people than any other group.

Some people feel a deep psychological guilt and insecurity about unemployment and seek, desperately at times, for a new job. Others may be only mildly interested in getting employment, particularly if the difference between social security and the wage of an unskilled job is small or non-existent; for these people it may be ultimate boredom which makes them eventually settle for a job. Others will be quite happy to remain idle as long as social-security benefits are available; they may in fact be able to supplement their social-security income by unnotified and therefore untaxed jobs. For such people it is easy enough to appear to be unattractive propositions to a potential employer. Yet other groups are frankly unemployable, with criminal records which effectively bar them from what appear to be appropriate jobs, or suffering from emotional instability, low intelligence, or general undesirability as far as prospective employers are concerned. Even if only one person in a hundred came into one of the last categories that would represent a quarter of a million registered as unemployed who may well be almost unemployable, although not officially distinguished from anyone else.

It is impossible for an overworked official in a Department of Employment office to read the minds of every man and woman who registers as unemployed and draws social security. Only the chronic and blatant malingerer or the palpably certifiable mental misfit is likely to be rejected at first glance; it is only too easy to settle for the test that if a person says that he wants a job then he is officially registered and goes into the statistics.

From this one might argue that the numbers of unemployed are exaggerated by the administrative process. But if on one side special factors and unmeasurable attitudes tend to inflate the numbers who register as unemployed, there are probably many more factors on the other side which ensure that the numbers registered as unemployed are more likely than not an under-estimation of the true scale of unemployment, particularly during a recession.

One obvious cause of numbers of unemployed being under-estimated arises from individuals who have lost jobs but do not qualify for unemployment benefit. Examples of this category include men and women who have been unemployed for a long time: a year's continuous unemployment is an administrative watershed. Anyone who either did not qualify or did not wish to undergo some form of means test to secure other social-security benefits might simply stop registering after this point: some of these people might be above the legal retirement-pension age, and though they did not wish to retire found they had little choice. Another major example is of the married woman who has paid no employee's contribution to social security, relying on her husband's cash contribution for retirement benefits. For married women in this situation, there is no financial incentive to register, since they cannot draw unemployment benefit; the fact that it may not be worth their while to register does not mean that they are not willing and ready to work.

Finally there can be a large number of people, the retired, the handicapped, married women, and others who would work, given the right conditions and the right level of remuneration. It is misleading to regard people as being willing or unwilling to work *in vacuo*, so to speak. No one really knows how many people would work given the right conditions, because the number is not a constant or indeed a verifiable figure. Conventionally, however, without postulating conditions vastly different from those prevailing in Britain today, it may well be that the figures of unemployed would have to be raised by a third or more to give a realistic assessment. Both the 1966 and 1971 Population Censuses showed that there was a substantial discrepancy of about one-third between people who regarded themselves as unemployed, for purposes of filling in a Census form, but who did not register as unemployed. Even that figure of one-third is very tentative in view of the uncertainties about why so many jobs have disappeared in recent years without unemployment figures rising correspondingly.

The fact that the numbers of registered unemployed, even allowing for the unemployable, probably significantly underestimates the true figure has a number of interesting implications.

In the first instance it is arguably a loss of productive resources which the country can ill afford.

Significantly however, although it has untoward economic effects, it probably has few political consequences. Governments are judged on the numbers of registered unemployed. There does not appear to be much mileage for the political opponents of a government in arguing that registered numbers do not fully state the true situation on unemployment. This is probably a comfortable situation for the government, particularly since the non-registered unemployed are almost by definition quiescent or resigned to the situation. There is therefore no very obvious political compulsion to solve the situation; and since governments are rarely short of more pressing issues, the issue is never really resolved.

But the nub of the matter is that the non-registered unemployed have not really gone away. They are still employable, in some instances more employable than the registered unemployed, and thereby lies a source of difficulty in controlling the economy. For if a government takes action to cure unemployment by reflation or more directly by creating jobs it is not necessarily the registered unemployed, the political sore thumb, so to speak, who take the jobs. The reverse of the earlier phenomenon may appear, i.e. very substantial reflationary measures will have been taken with no very obvious effects on the employment situation. And it is a sad but relevant political fact that few people really care whether there are 25,000,000 or 25,250,000 people in employment. They do care whether the unemployed figure stands at 500,000 or 250,000.

Job Vacancies

It has been suggested that job vacancies present a more accurate picture of the employment situation than unemployment. But the same sort of administrative problem between real and registered numbers arises here also. Employers seeking new workers do not have to register their vacancies and file them through the Department of Employment. Rightly or wrongly, employers may on occasion feel that they are not getting the right calibre of skilled workman or woman through the official channels. Even more does this apply to clerical, secretarial or executive staff, and the extensive network of private job agencies who vet applications and can charge employers a fee for placing this type of personnel shows that there is a substantial demand for non-official employment and recruiting agencies. Moreover, men and women may not wait till they are sacked before seeking new jobs and in this sort of situation will probably arrange their own placing directly and in advance so that the vacancies do not necessarily appear. Jobs are advertised, formally in newspapers, or even simply by a notice outside a works or factory. The total effect is that here too the total number of registered vacancies is probably an underestimate of the potential of jobs which really exist.

In summary then there is a difference between statistical appearance and reality in employment; this is, of course, true of most official statistics in any country – probably, however, figures are most unreliable in this particular field of manpower.

Is there a Pool of Unemployment?

Political commentators, and the man in the street who has never been unemployed or has only vague recollections of a transitory experience, often tend to think of the unemployed as being a fairly static group, particularly during a depression. This may have been true in the days of mass unemployment in the 1930s, and even today in regions of dying or dead industries. But for most parts of the country the picture of unemployment is far from being static.

Most people who lose or give up their jobs are unemployed for a relatively short time. This short-time or 'frictional' unemployment, while distressing for the people involved, is not a serious issue at national level. Indeed, one can say that this type of unemployment is necessary if there is to be any industrial mobility. Arguably, too, frictional unemployment of this type is likely to rise in prosperous times since people are willing to risk changing jobs with reasonable expectations of getting new and perhaps better jobs fairly quickly.

Thus, to say that the unemployment figure has been around one million for a year does not mean that the same million people have been out of work for this time. It means that several million have changed jobs willingly or otherwise; that a good many have done so without registering as unemployed at all, going directly from one job to another; that two or three million have registered as unemployed and have been, for a few weeks or even in some instances a few months, actually unemployed, and that there has been a hard core – some in very hard-hit regions, the elderly, the unadaptable, the unskilled, or those with wrong skills, in a proportion of instances the unemployable – out of work for a year. Most unemployed people are re-employed within two months, and only about one person in every five or six is out of a job for a year or more; this proportion scarcely varies from boom conditions to depression. An increase in unemployment in this sense can mean one of two things: more people losing their jobs, or people taking longer than usual to find – or take up – new jobs. If anything, the tendency under present-day circumstances is probably for people to take rather longer to get the type of job they want; certainly the economic sanctions to get any sort of employment are no longer as savage as they were a generation ago. There is some evidence that as unemployment and other social-security benefits rise, so does the length of time that individuals will be ready to remain unemployed – a not entirely surprising conclusion.

The fact that the static pool of long-term unemployed is probably relatively small compared with the total registered at any one time has important consequences. One is that, in periods of uncertainty, people will be less willing to change jobs, and that a slowdown in turnover of jobs may be a sign of anxiety about the future rather than a real indication of job satisfaction.

Clearly, although there are politically embarrassing implications to unnecessarily prolonged frictional unemployment the costs to the national economy may be relatively small. The suspicion however that increased social security benefits now available may create a problem of unnecessary unemployment, on occasion disguised as sickness, is something that may just have to be accepted as part of the price of the welfare state.

Types of Longer-term Unemployment

There is more than one type of longer-term unemployment: since the appropriate measures to deal with the situation vary it is important to be able to define the type of unemployment in any particular situation.

Conventionally longer-term employment can be divided into three types, structural, regional and cyclical: this is a useful threefold division with two provisos, namely that different people mean different things by the terms, and that the divisions are not always clear-cut and mutually exclusive, i.e. structural and regional unemployment may cover the same basic situation on occasion.

Structural unemployment is the term used in the general sense of an industry or a particular skill going into decline, either because the original factors which led to the establishment of the industry no longer apply, or because technology has overtaken existing methods in the industry. A coalmining area which is running out of coal seams is an example of the first; the replacement of coal-burning power stations by oil or nuclear power is an example of the second.

If the whole industry is in decline, e.g. the already quoted coal industry, shipbuilding, cotton textiles, or certain types of traditional heavy industry, then the problem of unemployment spreads across the entire range of skills involved. This is a situation which gives rise to a good deal of personal misery for the people who are being thrown out of jobs. Often industrial strife, when it arises in this situation, is directed not against the management as such (after all, they may be in the same boat) but against the government or even in a sense the whole technological process which causes the situation to arise. There is often in this situation a vested interest embracing both management and workers to bring pressure on the government somehow to avert, slow down or reverse the process of obsolescence by protection from competition, subsidy and the like. Rarely however is the object of such an exercise spelt out. There is almost always a specious argument that such action to reverse the trend of technology is desirable because the decline is only temporary. Unfortunately though, face-saving clichés of this sort are adopted, and all the parties concerned, management, workers and even government, can end up believing, often in the face of the facts, that one more extension of protection, one more subsidy from the public purse will somehow cure a lame duck. It rarely, if ever, does. The key issue for lame ducks of this sort is that the technological arguments can be subordinated to the political ones of cutting down unemployment by subsidy.

A more limited type of structural unemployment is the situation where a particular skill within an industry becomes replaceable, even when the industry as a whole remains viable. This is an area in which trade union attempts to preserve jobs and skills by demarcation disputes can be particularly acute. Conflict is often inter-union : it is not unknown for the conflict to arise within sections of the same union.

The main problems which a government faces in dealing with general or particular redundancies, i.e. within an industry or within a particular section, are obvious in economic terms; the solutions, in political terms, are not.

The immediate issue is whether to delay the rundown at the risk of perpetuating a sick industry or trade, until larger-term solutions can be found. The problem is usually compounded by the fact that in so many instances the industries or jobs which are being phased out are in the older industrial areas with their scars physical or emotional, of earlier industrial conditions. The long-term solutions, which will be discussed later, are to introduce new industries. It is difficult enough at any time to attract new industries into dying areas; when the short-term struggles and industrial disputes, intended to win central government support, or to win new areas at the expense of other trades, blow up into national crises, the long-term prospects are dimmed by the arguments about the short-term solution.

Regional unemployment is in some ways an overlap with the first type because, as it happens, many of the dying industries tend to be away from the present economic centre of gravity, namely the Midlands and the south-east.

If one plots percentage unemployment figures by region there is, generally speaking, a very high correlation between the distance from London and the level of unemployment. It is highest in Scotland, Ulster, Wales and Cornwall and progressively lessens as we move towards the centre, i.e. London. The relationship is by no means perfect; there are patches and variations, but the overall pattern is there. The pattern becomes more striking if it is seen as the part of a whole West European phenomenon. Here the pattern is repeated with the peripheral areas including not merely the areas in the United Kingdom but the whole of Ireland, the Brittany peninsula, Spain, Portugal, southern Italy, Sicily, Yugoslavia, Greece and Turkey. The role of these areas seems progressively to be to supply manpower to the industrial heart of Europe, the so-called 'Golden Triangle' from the Midlands of Britain across to the industrial conurbations of Belgium, Holland, the Rhine and Ruhr valleys and the Paris basin. Again the correlation is not perfect: there are pockets, whole areas, of industry with smaller centres elsewhere, but the golden triangle is the true industrial heart of Europe, and efforts to plant new industry, preserve old ones, and create new employment require vast investment: the further the region is from the centre, the more difficult and more expensive the process.

The reasons for this state of affairs are complex but some are readily identifiable. There is a snowball effect in industry: settled industry builds up over time its own ancillary services, an infrastructure with all the external economies of size. Success attracts success and other things being equal new industry will be drawn

in, attracted by the facilities and in turn providing more
facilities.

The industries which in the past became established in what
have since become the peripheral areas tended to do so for sound
industrial or geographical reasons: reasons, however, which
tended to become less important. Heavy engineering, shipbuilding, and mining tended to be located where the raw material
or geographical conditions dictated. In many instances the
original raw material sources became exhausted, although for a
time the inconvenience of having to bring supplies in from far
away tended to be compensated for by the external economies
which had been built up, merely by the industries having been
located in one particular region for a generation or two.

In the long run, however, the industrial base of the region
tended to be eroded by the emergence of new industries and
technologies with few of the constraints of the earlier industries.
Using less raw materials with power which could be piped in
virtually anywhere, these industries gravitated to newer and more
congenial areas. The decay and loss of ancillary services, the
reversal of the 'snowball' effect in the older regions, accelerated
the process.

With these older regions scarred by earlier industrialisation,
decaying industry bringing industrial unrest, many of the
younger, more ambitious or more able workers moving to more
pioneering areas, there is no very obvious reason to anticipate
economic recovery in many of these regions – rather yet more
regional unemployment.

The fact that aid is in many instances pumped in by the
central government seems at best to stem the slow haemorrhage
of jobs from these regions, not actually to cure the condition.

Regional unemployment is, arguably, another way of looking
at structural unemployment in obsolescent industry, i.e. structural
unemployment with a new dimension which accentuates the ills
of the situation by bringing about a situation where a whole
community, rather than a single industry within the community,
suffers. In another sense too, regional unemployment is one
dimension of the problem of a fair share-out of national
wealth, one of the objectives which will be discussed later.

Cyclical unemployment is the final type of long-term unemployment in the classification. An area in economic theory which

has attracted a good deal of attention in the past has been the phenomenon of the trade cycle, the apparently inevitable rhythmic movement of economic activity from boom to depression and back to boom again over a period of years, sometimes seven, sometimes nine or longer, The fluctuations of demand for goods expressed by this cyclical movement produced after the usual lag a cyclical movement in the unemployment figures.

A good deal has been written on the subject over the last half century or more and it is not proposed in an elementary exposition such as this to review the various analyses, particularly since it is only the consequences in terms of unemployment with which we are concerned. One point however has to be made. As long as there appeared to be inevitability in the cycle then it could be assumed that no boom or slump would last indefinitely. It was only when the slump of the 1930s showed no signs of ending and Keynes's explanation of the phenomenon in terms of investment implied that any conditions including a slump could in theory be sustained indefinitely, according to the level of investment, that fresh thought was applied to the earlier *ad hoc* measures of public works to relieve unemployment.

Out of the Keynesian approach came the idea of counter-cyclical expenditure, the idea of timing whatever public-sector spending could be advanced or retarded, so that it was at a maximum during depressions and a minimum during a boom. In other words demand would be ironed out into a more constant pattern so that slumps or excessive booms could be avoided.

There are any number of criticisms which can be made of the Keynesian explanation and the remedies suggested. Nevertheless even at the risk of a *post hoc, propter hoc* explanation in the post-war period the incidence of cyclical activity, including cyclical unemployment, has been damped down, particularly so far as slumps are concerned. But it would be wildly optimistic to assume that they had been eliminated from the post-war world : manifestly they have not, although their effects so far as the general public are concerned have been very subdued – possibly because until very recently employers were unwilling to shed unused labour during a depression.

There is still, in spite of Keynes, some indication of cyclical activity – shorter and shallower than pre-war but still apparently inevitable. The observable cycles are

1952–8
1958–63
1963–6
1966–71

The problem of cyclical unemployment is therefore in one sense a by-product of the general trade cycle, but with one very important difference since 1966 : that is in the willingness of employers to shed labour in a way which would not have been contemplated in the first two decades since the war.

How far does the concept of counter-cyclical spending work? The short answer is that it works very well – in time. If there is no external constraint or increased public sector spending (i.e. excessive inflation or a balance-of-payments crisis) then such expenditure, together with incentives to encourage increased investment or consumption in the private sector, is the answer. The main problem is the psychological one. If large numbers of people are convinced that the immediate economic prospects are poor, and adjust their behaviour accordingly, then the economic prospects will be poor – the classical example of the self-fulfilling prophecy discussed previously. The consequence will be that increased consumer spending simply will not take place and the restimulation of demand – the obvious riposte to a dip in the trade cycle – will be confined almost entirely to public sector spending. And the type of public sector spending which will be efficacious in creating large numbers of jobs will not necessarily make much sense economically.

Curing Long-term Unemployment

As with so many other problems in economics, the theoretical cure to unemployment is easy to find, but difficult to apply.

The problem of unemployment in the 1970s is that it is not, curiously enough, a mass homogeneous problem, but a selective one, one acute only in regions. While powerful remedies are at hand they are too unselective. By analogy one might say that selective unemployment is like a head cold, a good deal less harmful than the pneumonia of mass unemployment but rather more difficult to remedy.

What are the theoretical answers?

For *structural unemployment* there are two lines of action which can be followed. First, to decide whether a temporary tempering of the harsh realities for the industries concerned is possible or justified, and secondly to retrain personnel to other industrial skills.

The difficulty with the first part of the programme is purely political. A subsidy or some other form of aid may be justified on some grounds, or even on occasion on economic grounds, if it can be shown that the multiplier effects of letting an industry die off suddenly will outweigh the immediate cost of subsidising it. In practice however what tends to happen in a sick industry which receives a government subsidy, wiping off past debts, etc., is that a new vested interest is created. When it becomes clear that an industry is not going to be allowed to collapse, that the government is in effect offering a blank cheque to keep it going, then there is no obvious sanction on the part of management or workers to remedy the situation in the industry.

The alternative line of action is to retrain redundant men and women. In the long run this is the only sensible answer. In the short run there are again very difficult problems, both technical and political. The first need is to anticipate what fresh skills will be needed so that the retrained work-people will get jobs. Nothing is more demoralising than being retrained only to find that jobs are not available in the new skills or that they too become obsolescent fast. And in a technological dynamic society there are few skills which can guarantee a lifetime's employment. But at least as important is the attitude of existing workers in expanding industries to an influx of retrained workers – 'dilutees' is the word used in practice. In spite of protestations about the brotherhood of man it is a sad fact that where jobs require skill, trade unions are going to protect the interests of the original members, even if this means that other workers are going to be kept out. In the typical situation where no dilutee can be employed unless and until it can be proved that all existing tradesmen have jobs, regardless of suitability or competence, then the effect is that most really skilled trades stay closed to retrained personnel.

Regional unemployment, in so far as it can be distinguished from structural unemployment, is the most difficult of the three to overcome. The issue of regional development will be discussed in a later chapter but the main problem is that most measures designed to attract new industries or retain existing industry, spill over out of the regions which are supposed to benefit. In other words any subsidy, boom or grant which creates long-term employment opportunities is likely to have most effects elsewhere. To pour in sufficient aid to cure the unemployment problems of the regions is only too likely to cause excessive inflationary pressure elsewhere. The most effective method of curing unemployment in the short term is to commission public sector employment, build new roads, schools, hospitals, clear derelict land, etc. – all very helpful in creating a pleasant environment and providing a lot of temporary semi-skilled or unskilled employment, but essentially stop-gap short-term activities which do not generate momentum for further developments once the grants, and the obvious improvement projects, run out.

Cyclical unemployment represents a deficiency in demand spreading over the entire range of industry and ought therefore to be susceptible to reasonably unselective measures to increase overall demand. Again the measures may be of two sorts.

The first of these is an increase in public sector spending, but this time without too much regard to the location. The most appropriate type of spending is that which is likely to have a multiplier effect.

There is an excellent theoretical case for having a number of projects 'on the shelf' which can be brought into operation whenever the deficiency in demand appears. Unfortunately projects which are simultaneously worth while and yet can be postponed conveniently, for years if necessary, are not easy to identify in any quantity. What tends to happen is that, in a period of cyclical unemployment when political pressures begin to mount, governments are more likely to scratch around to find projects. In the end the projects which do emerge are of somewhat doubtful worth, and moreover take so long to produce any multiplier effect that the original cyclical situation has become irrelevant.

The second approach is to stimulate demand at the other end, consumer demand. This has the advantage of being speedier, but the disadvantages of being transient, i.e. a consumer boom which peters out before it has produced an accelerator effect of stimulating new investment.

There are in turn two approaches to the problem of creating a consumer boom. The orthodox method is simply to cut taxes, particularly taxes on consumption, and make up any deficit by borrowing. Ideally, of course, the tax cuts will be of the 'demand rich' variety, i.e. cuts which will be rapidly translated into increased spending. This means cuts in income tax, preferably at the lower end of the tax bracket where the marginal propensity to consume will be highest – in simpler everyday language, putting more purchasing power into the hands of the less well off. An alternative might be to increase social security benefits particularly on retirement or disablement pensions, because this again generates fresh consumption fast. The political problem about the latter is that such a shift in the distribution of national income tends to be in political terms permanent, and any immedate benefit to the economy has to be reckoned against the prospect of permanently committing the economy to making an increased share of the national income available for pensions. Some readers might well argue that this would be socially an excellent point; but the point here is that the economic argument is by no means as clear cut, and if the decision is made to put the social case before the economic one, it ought to be done as a long-term decision or policy, not as a temporary expedient with permanent results.

A rather unorthodox method, which would have the merit of giving a temporary boost of this nature without irrevocable social commitments for the future, is the 'bonus' payment, e.g. an extra two or three weeks' pensions to the retired in order temporarily to stimulate the economy in a pump-priming operation. By analogy rather like the use of so-called gift vouchers on detergents as a means of cutting prices temporarily so that one avoids the odium of raising prices, having once lowered them, simply by not issuing any more vouchers.

The difficulties about such a proposal are once again in the main political. Governments rarely have time for long-term contingency planning on the economic front, and serious discussions on this, as on capital projects 'on the shelf', simply do not get detailed discussion until a crisis situation develops. In this situation such a move, even if it were administratively possible at short notice, would be politically unacceptable if it appeared to smack of panic. Perhaps a government which made contingency plans for such a bonus and announced, well ahead of any crisis, that as and when the capacity of an economy was being substantially underutilised additional *ad hoc* bonuses would be made then the machinery would be prepared well in advance of another cyclical depression.[1]

Finally in this situation it is as well to remember that measures to stimulate demand are in this context meant to reduce unemployment; they can however produce alternative and undesirable results. It might well be that any additional purchasing power went into savings in a greater proportion than anticipated because people were apprehensive of the future, i.e. putting money away against a 'rainy day'. Demand-rich tax cuts are then not so demand-rich after all. Even more disconcertingly it may be that a sudden increase in purchasing power catches local manufacturers unaware – especially if their expectations are gloomy. In this situation a stimulation of demand will be met by a surge of imports, or by a rise in prices which is unjustified in terms of changing costs.

Other Proposed Solutions

There are at least two methods which are widely suggested as a means of curing unemployment. These are shorter hours and earlier retirement.

The argument for shorter hours is basically that if, for example, the average 40-hour week were cut tomorrow to 35, then unemployment would disappear. The main fallacy about this argument is that the advocates assume wages will not be cut accordingly. A 14 per cent wage increase or thereabouts would be the first stage, but only the first stage. Clearly unless wages and other related costs were to be cut so that the extra labour would cost no more than the original wages bill, it is hard to see how such a solution would be anything but another massive boost towards inflation.

In fairness to the advocates of this solution they are likely to argue that increased wages would stimulate demand and so

---

[1] The idea of a Christmas bonus for pensioners was introduced in 1972 by a Conservative government, not particularly as a cure for unemployment but rather to make its prices and income freeze by that time more acceptable. Previously this had been a 'once for all' bonus by the previous Labour government to cover an administrative gap.

raise output – an argument which may or may not be valid but where the beneficial effects if any are likely to be small compared with the inflationary implications.

The second point about the argument which requires closer examination is the frankly pernicious situation regarding overtime working in the United Kingdom. In spite of a steady progression of cuts in the official working week over the post-war years, it is noticeable that the actual hours worked in most industries have not fallen proportionately. As has been suggested earlier, the main object of pushing for a shorter working week may not be to cut hours but to push up wages by getting on to overtime and overtime rates as soon as possible. In many industries the official wage rates are virtually meaningless because of overtime rates and associated bonuses.

The practice of overtime wages as a perquisite of many jobs is condoned by many employers who in effect guarantee overtime. It is difficult to avoid the conclusion that the effect of cutting the official week in an industry from say 40 hours to 35 would be that the actual hours worked on average fell from say 48 to 44, i.e. a slight fall in hours compared with the increase in overtime rates, at probably much more than the 14 per cent increase originally envisaged. It is curious that in very many instances the argument is put forward that overtime ought to be taxed at a lower rate to encourage greater production in the United Kingdom. In practice a heavier tax rate on overtime might in the long run make for more efficiency by compelling employers to plan output more efficiently, and incidentally cut out the incentive mentioned in the last chapter for workers to spin out a job to make for more overtime.

There is a rather more valid reason for suspecting that the practice of regarding overtime as normal does affect the level of unemployment when industrial activity begins to pick up. Because of the overhead costs of extra labour, principally in terms of a fairly hefty national insurance contribution, the initial reaction of employers may be to step up the level of overtime rather than to take on extra labour, and this may create an inertia which has to be overcome before employment begins to pick up. The situation was even more liable to occur when the Selective Employment Tax was in operation. Conversely the slack in the system works in the other direction, in that an initial response to slacker conditions may be to reduce overtime. It might make more economic sense to save the national insurance contribution by dismissing redundant workers, but in fact this does not seem to happen – a situation encouraged by the readiness of trade unionists in many instances to share out the work, even to the extent of part-time working, to help out those fellow-workers who might otherwise lose jobs. The tendency to cut overtime and even normal hours as an alternative to sacking is also reinforced by the prospect of having to make redundancy payments.

It is frankly difficult to estimate at what point an employer will cease to use discretion about hiring or sacking employees using the margin afforded by variable overtime. This however is one of those instances of uncertainty, even non-economic behaviour, which makes it so difficult to predict accurately just how many extra jobs will be created by injecting increased demand into the economy by any of the traditional methods outlined in the first section.

The second argument advanced as a means of reducing employment is earlier retirement. In this instance many of the same arguments apply. Almost certainly, a once-for-all decision, involving solving a temporary deficiency in demand but a permanent change, is a risky option.

Additionally, in this instance there are the economic and social problems of putting men and women on the scrap heap, so to speak, before they want to retire or are incapable of working further. In spite of most people's protestations about their looking forward in their later years to retirement, it is probable that many, perhaps most, people dread the change and the inevitable cut in living standards which come about. Certainly for many men at sixty-five (and even more women at sixty) retirement comes as a psychological change for which they are ill prepared.

If earlier retirement were imposed, the standard of living of the individuals concerned would be drastically reduced, and the burden of increased social security costs on the remaining work force would be substantial. Although of course resolutions are regularly passed at trade union conferences demanding higher benefits as well as earlier retirement, and indeed threatening industrial action to this end, at the risk of being cynical few if any of the resolutions suggest that the trade union members concerned should have their own standards of living reduced to make the transfer payments available on the massive scale involved.

The difficulty about the shorter working week or earlier retirement as a solution for unemployment is that the easy gimmick is rarely costless. This is not to say that there is not an excellent case for reducing work hours (on a genuine as opposed to an overtime basis) and increasing the options of individuals to retire earlier than the present statutory limit; or conversely, if they are able and willing, to postpone retirement. Undoubtedly, as standards of living rise and automation reduces the need for manpower, it is possible to contemplate both possibilities of earlier or later retirement by individual choice. But the fact that these objectives are worth pursuing and adopting, as and when society can afford them, does not mean that they are the correct expedient for temporary demand difficulties. There is probably more room for experiment on breaking away from conventional 8-hour days for 5-day weeks to 3 or 4 days for semi-retired, or even 3-day weeks of 12 hours for some jobs if double shifts can be worked to use expensive capital equipment more thoroughly and this rather than shorter working weeks or early retirement might give more scope for creating more jobs along with increased production.

CHAPTER 6

THE DISTRIBUTION OF NATIONAL INCOME

THE division and distribution of national wealth is generally the key issue of domestic policy. This problem has several aspects of which the most immediately important is how far the distribution of national wealth and income will reflect political and economic power within the community; or how far action will be taken by the state to change this state of affairs, to redistribute income according to need, rather than power.

The Concept of a Compassionate Society

Over the past two or three centuries, as the United Kingdom has been transformed from an agricultural to an industrial society, two important sociological changes have taken place. The first of these has been a progressive weakening of family ties outside the immediate family. Putting this at its most cold-blooded, most citizens of the United Kingdom feel less and less economic responsibility for the support of their relatives, except for their own children during the period of dependency. At its most obvious this can be seen in the treatment of elderly relatives whose maintenance is often seen as a state responsibility rather than a family one. Pensions are paid on the assumption that the economically productive members of a society have little or no responsibility for their elderly relatives – a complete contrast to the extended family of other less developed parts of the world where the individual's duties extend not only to elderly parents but to remote cousins. Nepotism, frowned upon officially in western society, is a virtue elsewhere when it comes to promoting the welfare of any member of the family.

In contrast, however, to the weakening of individual responsibility there has been a remarkable extension of social responsibility. A relative indifference to suffering and hardship outside the family had been a characteristic of pre-industrial western society; it is a feature of many non-western societies, the obverse side of the concept of the extended family. By contrast in the United Kingdom today men and women are simply not allowed to starve to death in the streets.

This means that any British government, whatever its political complexion, now supports the principle of a welfare state ensuring at a minimum the provision of the necessities of life to all its citizens, healthy or ill, young or old, or for that matter deserving or undeserving if one may use a socially loaded term.

The welfare state implies a measure of redistribution of national wealth; the political argument in this country is not about the principle of the welfare state but how far welfare services should be extended and how they should be paid for.

Historically in the twentieth century the area of welfare and therefore the growth of transfer expenditure to this end has increased dramatically. It may be that a turning point will come in the future but, on present trends, welfare expenditure is more likely to expand than contract.

This has at least two important economic consequences. First, more and more national resources will be diverted by government action to welfare services, probably at the expense of private consumption. Transfer incomes both absolutely, and relatively as a proportion of public expenditure, are likely to rise.

Since this increase is likely to be at the expense of private consumption, purchasing power is being taken away from the better off who are better off because of their economic power. This group includes not only the rich and the professional classes, but the skilled tradesman. Thus the need for more taxation for welfare purposes means that the relationship between economic power and reward will be under constant review, indeed tension. Welfare expenditure is, almost by definition, a transfer from the economically productive (or powerful) to the economically unproductive, to bring about a distribution of national income that represents what society would regard as socially equitable rather than economically justified.

However the problems with which we are concerned are essentially economic or political, rather than a moral issue. There are some political facts of life which any government will have to face.

Virtually everyone is in favour of better pensions for the old or the disabled; political parties and conferences of trade unions will pass such resolutions almost as a ritual incantation. But in so far as this extension of welfare services is really a redistribution of national income virtually every group which favours such action expects the redistribution to be at somebody else's expense.

Trade unions in general support better conditions, including wages, for the less well off. A minimum national wage is also a regular incantation. But the skilled tradesman will resist attempts to close differentials in wages. Again therefore, in spite of the resolutions by trade unions in favour of the lower paid and less well off, the highly paid trade union member is just as unwilling as the rich *rentier* to sacrifice voluntarily part of his income. An increase in wages for the lower-paid worker inevitably means corresponding increases all along the line to maintain the differentials. If redistribution of income is desired, it will not in practice be achieved by trade unions agreeing to limit the wages of higher paid workers to aid the lower paid. It will come from government welfare schemes, not the voluntary abolition of wage differences.

Economic Efficiency and the Equitable Distribution of Income

It would be intellectually convenient if there was a clear relationship between economic efficiency and what would conventionally be regarded as an equitable distribution of income. Unfortunately the relationship is by no means clear, although there is some evidence that an excessively equitable distribution of income does limit incentive.

At one extreme one might conceive of a society where virtually all the effective purchasing power was controlled by a small section of the community. The recipients of this national income might spend it on personal pleasure, and the effects on the great mass of the population would be almost negligible; alternatively they might choose to invest it in capital projects designed to make the whole economy grow. But even if they followed the latter course, their intentions might be frustrated because there was so little effective demand for more production simply because the majority of the population were not effectively a part of the market. Growth requires not merely investment but a sustained demand for the products of the new investment.

At the other extreme one might conceive of an economy where

the state decided to redistribute income so that everyone, working, retired or idle, voluntarily or involuntarily, received the same income. The danger of such a situation is that there would be little incentive to work, seek promotion or make any great exertion. The incentive to make an effort, if there is any, then becomes non-monetary, perhaps social, perhaps ideological, perhaps just absent. This method has been tried by some socialist states 'From each according to his ability, to each according to his need' was a well-known phrase at an earlier political stage in the U.S.S.R. The general tendency has been however for a rather utopian approach to be dropped, as ideological fervour cools. Today there is probably a higher degree of equality of income in the United Kingdom than in the U.S.S.R.

The political decision for any government then is to distribute national income as equitably as political convictions permit, bearing in mind however the desirability on political grounds of keeping taxation as low as possible. Too heavy taxation is widely regarded as destroying initiative, and although the proposition is hard to prove empirically a widespread feeling of excessive taxation does seem to produce resentment and willingness among certain sections to opt out of extra effort. The worker settles for higher absenteeism – more leisure cannot be taxed – the executive seeks other non-taxable perquisites of office, the expense account, the company car and so on.

The point has already been made that all political parties, and the trade unions, pay lip-service to more equality. It would be pleasant to record that equitable redistribution of national income was practised as well as preached by individuals. In general however redistribution has to be done by governments, and in conflict with the interests of the better off, including in this category the higher-paid workers – or on an international basis the workers in a developed society as against the underdeveloped world.

An Incomes Policy

The concept of an incomes policy lies at the heart of the debate on equitable shares of national income. Incomes policy comprises both the issue of the distribution of factor incomes, i.e. wages, salaries, dividends and so on, but also factor incomes arising from pensions and other social security benefits. It is perhaps significant that when politicians and trade unionists talk about incomes policy they are thinking largely in terms of wages and dividends – with perhaps a token gesture towards the pensioners. Here, as elsewhere, the implication is that while everyone is in favour of more money for the old and the disabled, this is somehow a separate share-out from the other income sources.

If the public at large is willing to make approving sounds about increases for pensioners – provided the detail of how they are to be paid for is not spelled out – the same may be said about incomes policy – again provided the detail is not spelled out. The fact remains however that though incomes policy is excellent as a general principle, the nitty-gritty detail makes a practical long-term policy very difficult indeed.

We might start by considering one or two well-rounded phrases which tend to attract warm if vague approval, as a principle on which to base an incomes policy.

(a) *'Fair shares for all'* or possibly 'To each according to his needs'. The vague principal of 'fairness' attracts general approval – at least until one gets down to detail.

The first point which occurs is that such a principle as fairness or necessity is not likely to be the basis on which wages or other *factor* incomes are paid. People are paid what their employer (including in the public sector, the state as employer) reckons them to be worth – if necessary, with their worth being measured in terms of economic strength from time to time through industrial disputes. They are not paid equally or according to their individual circumstances. If a redistribution of income on the lines of equality or individual circumstance is then deemed desirable this is done by the state redistributing national income – e.g. by taxing the better off and redistributing to the needier. There is therefore the perennial conflict between reward according to economic worth (i.e. economic strength) and fair shares.

If the reader really imagines that many people subscribe to the concept of fair shares or payment according to need, he might care to reflect on the rigid determination of skilled trade unions, already remarked on, to maintain their wage differential over their less-skilled brethren. Time and time again an industrial dispute has been on the verge of settlement if only the lowest paid group of workers in dispute received a fairly modest increase in an offer, only for the negotiations to break down because a small increase to the least well off has got to be translated *pro rata* through the various grades: not, in fairness to the disputants, because a little extra money is all that important, but simply because the differential would be eroded if only the less well off were given an increase.

In the same way it is a political fact of some importance that certain social security benefits are notoriously unpopular with sections of the community not directly involved. An obvious way, for example, of reducing poverty among the lowest-paid sections of the community might be to pay increased family allowances to those with large families. But as more than one progressively minded social security minister has found out the hard way, the idea of paying increased benefits to the poor with large families is not a vote winner among the rank-and-file Labour Party and trade union member with a small family and a conviction that people with large families should expect to pay themselves for their families' upkeep. In certain key areas of redistribution of income, a large proportion of the community who would normally vote for the Left-wing party (and by implication more redistribution of national income) are just as reactionary as their Right-wing neighbours, and a good deal more reactionary than the political leaders of either of the major political parties.

Once the redistribution of income implied in fair shares, or to each according to his need, passes downwards from redistributing the income of the well-to-do, to the skilled or semi-skilled craftsman, resistance increases very rapidly.

(b) *Income according to contribution to the community* is another fairly fine-sounding sentiment. But the trouble about this approach is that the contribution to the community tends to be measured in terms of economic strength – and one's contribution to the community then tends to be settled by an economic free-for-all with those currently making little or no economic contribution to the community, the old, children, the sick, going to the wall. This is, of course, a vast injustice. It is equally a vast injustice that one's contribution to the community should inevitably be measured in economic terms, i.e. by definition, the most powerful make the most contribution and demonstrate the fact by the amount of national income they can appropriate. But economic power of this sort is about the only objective measure that can be devised, and a major role of the state is to mitigate this tendency by squeezing the most powerful in turn.

(c) *The 'comparability' argument*, which simply amounts to the idea that if one section of the community gets a percentage increase in income, then another section of the community can demand comparable treatment, i.e. if the miners get a 10 per cent wage rise, then power workers should get the same, so should railway workers, and so on. In spite of the manifest absurdities of the situation there is a certain political convenience in the argument.

The flaws are, however, obvious: it is an appeal to the *status quo*. Everyone is entitled to the share of the national income he has always had. People, of course, do not accept this proposition, at least if they, or their skills, are on the way up; moreover, there never has been a base-year time in recent years when every section of the community, or even merely the trade unions, would agree that the share-out had been just right. As a stop-gap version this enables a form of equitable settlement to be made. As a long-term solution to the problems of securing growth and technical advance it is palpable nonsense. The difficulty is that the short-term expedient tends to be extended until reality intrudes, possibly in the form of a demand from the most economically powerful section of the community that the rules be changed so that they got more than the 'norm', whatever that was.

A variant on this is to attempt a flat across-the-board increase in money, not in percentage terms: again obviously this is a form of redistribution in favour of the lower-paid workers against the higher-paid, in contradiction to the economic facts of life, i.e. the ability of the powerful to get more than the norm. It can work as a stop-gap measure, i.e. a temporary wage 'freeze' variant, but only as a stop-gap.

Is an Incomes Policy Inevitable?

The most important single factor in the distribution of national income in recent years has been the apparent rise in the power of the trade unions. This has not only had the effect of pushing up the share of national income going to wage-earners but has also substantially contributed to cost-push inflation. The unions as a whole have not been ready to agree among themselves on the share-out of national income among their members; but at the same time individual unions are powerful enough to secure equivalent rises in other unions, and so produce a leap-frog effect.

In such a situation the individual union, even if it were willing to restrain its own claims in the national interest, would hesitate to be the first to call a halt to the leap-frog process. A break in the progression has to be imposed from outside the system – and only the government now represents such a power.

It might seem reasonable to suppose that employers, individually or in organisations, would impose a bar, as they did in the past. In some way, however, either the power or the resolution of employers seems to have been eroded. There are a number of reasons for this, but at least two stand out.

As industry becomes more and more technologically advanced the proportion of capital equipment to labour costs goes up and up. At first glance this might suggest a weakening of the position of labour, but the reality is very different. If the cost of labour falls as a proportion then there are strong reasons why an employer will hesitate to bring about a stoppage by refusing even a large wage claim. A 10 per cent settlement would be a very serious cost if, for example, 90 per cent of the running costs of a firm were in the form of wages. But if wages form only, say, 25 per cent then the picture is altered.

The difficulty is, of course, that every individual settlement affects expectations and claims elsewhere. An individual employer might argue that his decision to pay a large settlement had little or no effect on the national picture; but the effects of thousands of such decisions by employers, each one of which is, on its own, insignificant, does create a climate for large-scale settlements – which incidentally are in time going to affect the cost of the capital equipment, which initially did not seem to be involved.

This is the sort of situation where what is good for the individual is bad for the economy as a whole. It can make sense for each employer individually to settle for a larger pay claim; the employer who stands out has a good deal to lose.

It may be possible for an employers' association to finance a stand by one of its members and encourage joint action to resist excessive claims. But arguably the employers as a whole are going to be chary about committing themselves to a head-on clash with the unions on an issue which they see as being the concern of the central government, not the employers.

Beneath the obvious clash of trade unions and employers there often exists an identity of interest as against the consumer, i.e. the public at large. Employers are liable, where they can, to avoid the confrontation if it seems possible to pass on the costs of increased wages by raising prices; ideally too they will adjust their profit margins in the process. In the circumstances it may well be that only the central government will represent the general consumer interest.

If the nature of modern industry often is to weaken the resolution of employers to resist large wage claims, the position of the striker has been strengthened at the same time.

The effect of going on strike is that a degree of hardship is suffered – but not necessarily an unsupportable one. The administrative machinery of taxation and social security are such that there is a vigorous attempt to avoid payment of social-security benefits on a national assistance basis. This is achieved by accelerating the repayment of taxes withheld by employers under the Pay As You Earn system. The amount of tax due falls automatically the moment earned income ceases and back taxes may be due for repayment in part. This repayment is speeded up, so that strikers will not claim social-security benefits – the repayment incidentally often being made by the employer against whom the strike is directed. So, for a week or two after the commencement of a strike, income in the form of tax rebates is guaranteed. When this begins to run out, the dependants of strikers will qualify for social-security benefits; officially the strikers, be they single or married, do not qualify. But the single man is likely to have the most tax rebate in any event, and no one seriously imagines that the wife of a striker who qualifies for social-security benefit will refuse to share food, shelter and warmth with the head of the family on the grounds that only the wants of the children and herself are being catered for.

Amendments to the present taxation and social-security system may in time reduce this apparent bias in favour of the whole social-security system becoming a potential source of strike pay. But a tender concern for the welfare of women and children has weakened the sanctions of hardship; no one starves during a strike.

The other point about strikes today is that they are very rarely followed immediately by dismissals. Individuals or groups of workers rarely lose their jobs as a result of a strike, because firms rarely collapse spectacularly during strikes. A strike is more

E

often than not simply a one-way option – if successful securing
a wage increase, if unsuccessful no wage decrease; and even
perhaps sufficient overtime at premium wage rates to make up
lost production, to the point that losses are just as likely as not
to be made up.

The answer is frankly conjectural, depending as it does largely
on the ability of the employers to pass on the costs to the public.
Ironically too the fact that British governments will permit
sterling to float, or even devalue drastically, rather than slow
down industrial expansion means that the discipline of increased
competition from abroad does not loom so large as the more
general effects of inflation. The ill-effects of a strike on the
country's economy no longer necessarily fall directly on the
industry involved but on the economy as a whole in terms of
increased inflation.

In a situation where employers may feel they have little to
gain and much to lose by resisting wage demands, and unions
conversely feel they have much to gain and nothing to lose by
pressing them, then an economic free-for-all becomes almost inevitable. Unless, that is, the central government steps in to resist
excesses in income rises.

In a sense all modern governments are constantly operating in
the incomes policy field, the moment they introduce any element
of progressive taxation or social security, for the simple reason
that such activities are already redistributing income away from
the pattern dictated by economic strength. Arguably, all that
happens when incomes policy becomes a declared government
aim is that the central government is being drawn further into the
field in which it is already operating, by the vacuum caused by
the retreat of the employers from the field.

Political Popularity

One of the most intriguing aspects of the situation is that while
most short-term solutions are economic nonsense in the long run,
they may be very acceptable politically in the short run. In a
crisis the great majority of the community will respond to an
appeal for fairness or moderation, as was demonstrated by the
popularity of a temporary wage freeze even among rank-and-file
trade unionists in the United States in 1971 and the United
Kingdom in 1972. Two factors were probably at work: first,

that if the individual was being asked to forgo an increase in income, so was everyone else, so that there was an element of justice; but equally perhaps an implication that since the measure was temporary, no long-term hopes of redistributing national income were being lost.

The difficulty is, of course, that temporary freezes come to an end – and the result may be that demands which have been delayed, pent up indeed, sweep away all the benefits of a freeze. There are thus two difficulties about imposing temporary incomes policies. The first is to get them started; the second is to stop them without disaster.

CHAPTER 7

A REGIONAL POLICY

THE problem of regional disparities has already been mentioned in terms of unemployment. But the situation can be summed up in the idea that in the United Kingdom as elsewhere in western Europe, there is a core of industrial activity which creates its own economies or diseconomies. New industries tend to be attracted into prosperous regions, where the appropriate infrastructure already exists, where ancillary services are available and where skilled labour can be found. If one is an industrialist contemplating building, say a new car plant, the obvious place to build is across the road from a rival plant, sharing facilities and poaching skilled labour. There are few incentives for building hundreds of miles away from existing facilities.

The tendency has, in recent years, been reinforced by the economics of the Common Market which have gone far to create an industrial heartland for western Europe, including the Midlands and south-east England. By implication the traditional industrial regions outside this heavy concentration begin to suffer from the snowballing of facilities in the centre area. Many of the industries of the peripheral areas are old-established and traditional owing their original siting to geographical factors such as local sources of raw materials or fuel which have since become exhausted. The outlying regions therefore are only too often areas of declining industries, the landscape and environment in general being scarred and polluted, with, in all probability, bad labour relations – all factors contributing to the process of decay.

There is, in this situation, almost inevitably a migration of the younger and more active members of the community. If, for social reasons, the central government wishes to stay, or reverse, the trend, it has to do so in the teeth of the economic realities. Almost inevitably the costs will be high and the results relatively disappointing. In the forty years or more in which the British government has tried to reverse the trend towards the south-east of England, the results have been frankly meagre. At most, the steady migration to the south-east has been slowed down. It has not been stopped, let alone reversed.

Reversing the Situation

So far as private industry is concerned the government has the choice of using stick or carrot, i.e. compulsion or incentives. Compulsion can only be negative, and consists essentially of licensing industrial development in prosperous regions, by requiring any expansion of existing facilities to be positively sanctioned. If, in theory, an industry is told that it will not be permitted to put up more plant in the Midlands or the south-east, it may, perforce, go to the less developed regions.

The stick of compulsion however has almost certainly got to be matched by the carrot of incentive and this means a financial incentive. There are a variety of methods available most of which have both advantages and disavantages. These can be summarised under three headings, namely investment grants, investment allowances and some form of wage subsidy.

The principle of investment grants is that a direct subsidy will be paid to a firm setting up in the so-called Development or Special Development Areas. This may run into millions of pounds in the case of say, an American multi-national corporation setting up a manufacturing subsidiary in Scotland. One of the earliest forms of such assistance was in industrial estates dating back before the Second World War where new factory buildings were erected with public funds and rented out at low cost to attract new industry into depressed regions. In recent years there has been no overall shortage of such accommodation and grants have tended to be a straight payment.

There are two problems attached to this policy. Grants are not related to efficiency or profitability, and the very generosity of the grant may be a disincentive to strive too hard for efficiency. The second point is that such financial aid favours the incomer but not existing industry in the regions which may be struggling for existence. Arguably it would have been a good deal cheaper to subsidise existing employment than try to create new jobs.

The argument about the wastefulness of investment grants was brought forward by the Conservative government in 1970; the grants were replaced by investment incentives operating via the tax system. Basically, these incentives were very generous tax

allowances against profits so that the more efficient and profitable
a firm in one of the assisted regions the more it would benefit.

The problems about incentives were again twofold. Like the
grants, they tended to favour the newcomer against the existing
firm, though not in such an extreme form if the latter firms could
achieve profitable expansion. More importantly in the event, as
government tax incentives were increased throughout the
economy in 1971 to encourage higher investment the differential
advantages of the assisted regions was largely eroded. By the
following year the government found itself supplementing the
new incentives, through a revised form of the tax grants, which
were in effect very similar to the grants abolished two years
earlier.

The final variant in the incentive scheme is some form of
wage subsidy. The regional employment premium introduced in
1967 by the then Labour government meant that in designated
regions employers would receive a wage subsidy. The scheme
covered about 20 per cent of the working population and applied
to all industry, old or new, in these regions. In order to give
continuity to industrial development an undertaking was given
that the system would last for a minimum of seven years, i.e. to
1974. The incoming Conservative government announced its
abolition from 1974, but left itself the option of replacing the system by something else. The 1974 Labour government renewed it.

It would probably be true to say that the Conservative govern-
men of 1970, disliking what it saw as the wasteful aspects of the
previous government's regional plans, tried to put more
emphasis on rewarding efficiency in the regions rather than
blanket subsidies. In the event however the unexpectedly
high level of unemployment which developed appears to have
forced a political if not an economic reassessment : the result was
a massive reversal of policy culminating in a new Industrial
Investment Act offering massive subventions (up to £550
million in the first instance) to prop up ailing industry or
introduce new ones in the Development Areas. It cannot really
be said however that in the early 1970s the drain of population
and industry from the regions had been stopped so far as private
industry was concerned.

Such incentives are intended to bring in private industry to
declining areas. It is of course a good deal easier to affect location

of industry in the public sector. It is however just as expensive in the long run.

First, publicly owned facilities, general civil service or nationalised industry administration groups, can in theory be located in regions of heavy unemployment by simple fiat; the main problem, however, is a human one. A civil servant resident in London may have considerable reservations about being banished several hundred miles away from the metropolis. Moreover the build-up of jobs must of necessity be slow, and the tendency therefore is to build up new facilities rather than attempt mass transfers of longer established services.

Moreover, in so far as the types of jobs created are mainly administrative or clerical, they are not particularly appropriate to replace traditional heavy industries : in fact female jobs form a high proportion of such vacancies, and as it happens are not the sort of jobs to absorb manual or semi-skilled workers in the heavy industries which are in decline.

The other area where the government can play a more direct role is by authorising more public sector spending in the development regions, e.g. provision of improved roads, schools, by housing grants, etc. All these are very worthy objectives in so far as they make the environment more attractive. Essentially, however, they are palliatives rather than remedies.

The Dilemma of Regional Development

There are two issues which have been left unresolved in regional development since the war : their existence may go a long way to explaining the relative failure of successive governments' efforts since the end of the war.

The most important is probably the conflict of aims in introducing modern industry. Modern industry is generally capital-intensive rather than labour-intensive : the more advanced the technology involved the less labour, particularly manual labour, is likely to be required. The result is that in proportion to the very heavy capital costs involved, a new industry requires a small number of highly skilled and technically trained people : in so far as manual labour is required, the premium is often on dexterity rather than physical strength and therefore female labour is the more appropriate. Indeed even the latter source of jobs may be a short-term development as the companies which do move into the

development regions are often subsidiaries of multi-nationals, and
the latter in many assembly industries are adopting the technique
of cheap assembly work in the underdeveloped world.

The effect is that, as with the public sector, appropriate jobs
for the displaced workers in the traditional industries, mining,
heavy engineering and the like are difficult to create in modern
industry. Thus the choice often boils down to subsidising
industries which are obsolescent or inefficient, and often strike-
ridden. Traditional industries and jobs are therefore kept in
existence, at a high cost; and as has been remarked earlier the
true nature of the operation is disguised by the political convention that in some indistinct future the industries will become
viable again. Once again, too, the result is a political palliative
but no real solution to the problem of creating new industry in
the region.

A second problem is that the effect of the various grants and
tax incentives, combined with the measure to limit expansion in
the more prosperous regions, is to ensure the creation of branch
factories rather than the main factories. Thus the regions become
more susceptible to an economic recession than the home regions,
for it is the branch factories which are liable to be put on short
time or closed down in a depression, not the main factory.

The implications of what might be described as the economic
expendability of the regions are profound, in political as well as
economic terms.

One issue which will have to be tackled more positively is the
radical concept of moving away from piecemeal measures which
attract marginal new industry in the form of branch factories.
If considerable public subventions are to be paid directly in the
form of grants, or indirectly in the form of allowances, then there
is a case for a global not a piecemeal approach – namely the need
to create a new industry or transfer an older industry from the
south-east as a whole, not merely settling for the branch factory
approach. There are obvious difficulties, both national and international, in moving away from dependence on branch factories.
But with public subventions to the regions now running to an
annual total of some £500 million, and the number of jobs
being created barely keeping pace with closures elsewhere, there
is need for a drastic revision.

Without such a change it is by no means easy to see a way out of the present regional problem, which has become a political hot potato no one really wants to handle. The result tends to be that to the inauspicious economic climate of the regions is added a deterioration of regional morale to the point that it is assumed that only by subsidy or some other form of protection can jobs be sustained. The result is frankly enervating so far as local initiative is concerned.

It may be possible to detect in the generally sombre background to the regional problem a somewhat uncertain gleam of light. To some extent the very advance of technology which has done so much to accelerate the drift from the outlying regions may, in the last quarter of the century, reverse the trend a little.

The practical inconveniences of living in the densely populated frenetic and very expensive south-east of the United Kingdom may be producing a more favourable appreciation of the merits of the less-populated regions, especially as the scars of early industrialisation disappear. A movement away from the densely populated regions becomes possible as executives begin to accept that it is practical to communicate more easily than ever before. Once televised meetings became a practical possibility the need for a permanent presence in London becomes less obvious. Other nations have avoided the dominance of a single economic centre like London, and a measure of dispersion may become the pattern for the future. But the proposition is frankly conjectural: the immediate problems may if anything be intensifying in the short run as a result of the very perceptible movement towards economic integration on a European scale.

The second source of light is that the only significant new discoveries of raw materials in the twentieth century, namely oil and natural gas, are occurring in the regions which need new industry and employment, i.e. off Scotland and in the Celtic Sea off Wales and the West Country. These regions which have experienced two or three generations of decline have at least the opportunity of a new generation of employment and affluence.

Economic Integration – the Implications for Regional Development

The point has already been made that the problem of unemployment and industrial decline in the United Kingdom is in many respects only the national aspect of a European problem of an industrial heart and less prosperous peripheral regions.

In the European context, however, some of these relatively depressed areas are separate nation states, e.g. Spain, Portugal or Greece, while others, like Brittany, south Italy and Sicily, are regions of nation states.

In what respect does national independence change the problem of the regions?

If a depressed region is also an independent state, the regional conditions will be expressed in a number of ways, only some of which will be common to the non-national regions.

In the first instance in a very real sense its G.N.P. per head of the population will be lower than that of the industrial countries of the centre. Frequently this discrepancy in G.N.P. level will be expressed in a devaluation of the national currency. There will be substantial unemployment, whose effects will be only partially alleviated by the devaluation, and a major source of its foreign revenue may well come from the export of workers to the labour-hungry centre – the outlying countries of Europe are the major source of the foreign labour, the 'guest workers' who have inherited the menial tasks in the prospering economies of the Common Market.

Thus in a sense an equilibrium is established between regions and the centre, on the basis that the former accepts a permanently lower standard of living than the latter, which, in a real sense, it serves.

If the region is just that, a region of a country, not a whole economy, then the same problems exist but yield different answers. As one example it is economically impossible for a lower standard of living in the regions to be accepted as inevitable, and signalled by devaluation. Regions cannot devalue in this sense: the nearest equivalent was the payment within the United Kingdom of regional employment premiums of up to £1.50 per worker introduced in 1967. Such a premium is a form of devaluation even if it is not called so.

But the fact that devaluation cannot take place is part of the larger problem that there is very strong economic and social pressure to prevent regional variations growing. Trade union pressure, for example, ensures that national wages, though not necessarily earnings, are uniform. But where unions have a minor role, e.g. in salaries to managers perhaps, or secretarial staff, there may be very substantial differences between the income of a manager or a shorthand typist in Glasgow or Belfast compared with London.

Thus, again an uneasy balance may be struck, whereby the logic of a lower standard of living for the outlying region is restrained by the political and economic pressures towards equal returns to the same types of labour throughout the economy. The balance, however, will persist only if there is a substantial and deliberate redistribution of national income towards the region. Notwithstanding the element of subsidy, by investment grants, social-security payments *et alia*, the characteristic of a declining region, the draining away of some of the most active labour force, will be a feature of the region as of the small country. Scots, Irish, and North Country workers and professional men, working in the Home Counties or the Midlands, are given a higher social rating than the Portuguese or Turkish 'guest worker' in Germany. But they are produced by the same forces.

What are the implications for the regions? Firstly for U.K. regions with potentially a non-English nationalist background, i.e. Scotland, Northern Ireland or Wales, there is a potential trade-off between the social and national satisfactions of political independence, and the possibility that the price of political independence might be a lower standard of living. Political independence for the Republic of Ireland has been bought at the cost of a lower standard of living. The fact that the price appears to be acceptable to the majority of nationals living in the Republic is perhaps a salutary reminder that not all decisions are made on economic grounds.

Thus one might reasonably argue that where a region has political independence it may have more room for manoeuvre, i.e. the option to devalue : but almost certainly it has a lower standard of living than it would have as a part of the political unit which extended into the industrial heartland of Europe, while a region without political independence enjoys many of the benefits of the industrial heartland, but at the expense of lack of control of its own destiny, economic or political. Economic independence for the British regions would probably be a chimera in any event. The Irish Republic, as its politicians are painfully aware, is still economically an appendage of the United Kingdom. The lack of political control however may be one of these ill-understood factors which have produced a feeling of, if not hope-lessness, at least of acceptance of economic backwardness by many of the industrialists and workers in the regions.

Such conjectures, however, cannot be proved, and for that reason might seem pointless in an economic discussion. There is however yet another dimension to the issue of regional develop-ment arising from British membership of the European Economic Community. E.E.C. regional policy has still to develop to a definitive stage. At the moment the policy amounts to little more than two principles :

(a) That members' national territories may be divided into two types, namely central areas where regional aid is very limited, and 'peripheral' areas where national governments can be much more lavish in providing aid : obviously in this situation much turns on how particular U.K. regions are classified.

(b) That aid must be 'transparent', i.e. readily measurable as a percentage of the cost of any investment in the regions.

In both instances the aid is being provided by the individual national government. It is theoretically possible to envisage a situation where organs or appendages of the Community struc-ture could be used to funnel in Community aid, e.g. the Coal and Steel Community might have a role to play in financing modernisation of these industries in the depressed regions. But in more general terms a Community regional policy has still to evolve to a definitive stage.

The evidence is that the U.K. government has more to gain than most from such a policy, if it were backed up by Community funds, and may therefore attempt to take a leading role in this development. But the implication is that even if more funds, national or Community, become available, the existence of a supranational authority may limit the options open to the U.K. government to deal with the U.K. regional problems.

CHAPTER 8

PRICES – INFLATION AND DEFLATION

The problem of large and long-term fluctuations in price levels (or to put it another way, changes in the value of money) is a problem which has occurred spasmodically throughout history. The present form of the problem, inflation, has been present for over thirty years, and has been fairly acute for the past few years. Inflation however is not the only possible form of the problem – the converse, deflation, has been encountered in the past and may recur in the future.

It may be helpful to look at changes in the value of sterling since the outbreak of the First World War (see Table 6, p. 142).

There have been three distinct phases during this period:

(a) A period of inflation during and immediately after the First World War. Almost certainly this was a period of very rapid growth of national income beyond the point of inflation – indeed inflation was a world-wide problem during the period.

(b) Most of the 1920s and the first half of the 1930s. This was a period of deflation, deliberate during the 1920s, rather more unplanned after that. The deliberate policy was occasioned by the desire to raise the value of sterling as a prerequisite of returning to the pre-war gold standard, and the subsequent attempts to maintain the new value. In the 1930s the deflation was a by-product of the world slump.

(c) A steady rise immediately before, during and after the Second World War. Figures for the actual war are largely meaningless because of the severe rationing of the period. There has been a marked acceleration since the middle 1960s.

In both inflation and deflation there is a tendency to redistribute national income.

Although deflation has been a problem and may become so again it is a rather more artificial situation than inflation. Not only was it less common in the period under discussion, but for about two-thirds of the time was a result of deliberate policy. Inflation, in contrast, is more easy to slip into, unplanned, and in moderation may have some political advantages.

TABLE 6

INDEX OF PURCHASING POWER OF THE POUND STERLING 1914–73
(*1963 = 100*)

Year	Index number	Year	Index number
1914	485	1946	184
1915	394	1947	172
1916	332	1948	160
1917	275	1949	156
1918	239	1950	152
1919	225	1951	139
1920	195	1952	131
1921	215	1953	129
1922	265	1954	127
1923	279	1955	122
1924	277	1956	117
1925	275	1957	114
1926	282	1958	111
1927	289	1959	110
1928	292	1960	109
1929	296	1961	106
1930	307	1962	102
1931	329	1963	100
1932	337	1964	97
1933	346	1965	93
1934	344	1966	89
1935	339	1967	87
1936	330	1968	83
1937	314	1969	79
1938	311	1970	75
Wartime rationing		1971	70
and controls		1972	66
invalidated the indices		1973	61

Thus far, inflation has been defined only in very loose terms. It is now worth while considering in rather more detail what is involved in inflation, since it is, in the 1970s, one of the major preoccupations not merely of the United Kingdom, but most of the world.

The first approximation of a definition used so far was 'too much money chasing too few goods'. This definition however raises almost as many issues as it solves – what exactly is meant

by money, for example, how we measure the amount of it in cir-
culation, and why in a situation of an economy with substantial
spare capacity does it prove so difficult to match the output of
goods to the supply of money, or vice versa.

It must be admitted that the problem of inflation, as it exists
today, is inadequately understood. It is as well to remember the
point previously noted that inflation (like deflation) tends to be
an international phenomenon and in that sense is only partly
amenable to action by individual governments. Large economies
can and do export inflation or deflation to the rest of the world.

To take an extremely crude example, if, as has happened in
the past, inflation exists in one of the very large economies like
the United States, it is possible to follow out the consequence in
terms of the crude model of injections and leakages developed
earlier.

Inflation involves a growing demand for goods and services.
This will draw in imports to meet demand. Imports are one form
of leakage of purchasing power and will tend therefore to
dampen down the inflation within the economy, even if no other
action is taken by the government concerned to restrain inflation.

But from the point of view of other countries the increase
in exports they experience as U.S. imports rise will constitute a
multiplier which will have untoward effects if the economies are
anywhere near full working capacity. If, of course, these countries
have spare capacity they will welcome the export-led boom, at
least up to the point where full employment is approaching and
a rise in monetary income takes over from real growth. Thus they
will experience inflation by the very process which is relieving the
U.S. inflation. The United States is in fact exporting inflation.

The actual implications of the model go a good deal further
but it is possible, even with an extremely crude model like this, to
see that inflation rapidly becomes an international problem.

The process works in reverse too – exporting deflation from the
large powers to the smaller – and this helps to explain why the
U.S. slump of 1929 had, within two years, become a world slump.

In recent years both the United Kingdom and the United
States have been accused by the financially orthodox finance
ministers and bankers of western Europe of exporting inflation
by running substantial balance-of-payments deficits – an excel-

lent example of the interdependence of modern economies and the ease with which, unwittingly, the actions of one national economy have repercussions elsewhere. Thus, when the world economy overall is expanding rapidly, then a nation which is too successful in exporting may create inflation with its own territory through the export multiplier; if, on the other hand, it runs a deficit in its foreign trade it may be exporting a measure of inflation.

The international implications are, of course, far more complex than thus far explored but the two factors which matter most in this context are :

(*a*) It is probably impossible for a nation to eliminate inflation (or for that matter deflation) on its own account if the condition is widespread internationally, unless it chooses to isolate itself completely from the world economy.

(*b*) In spite of the interdependence of economies, nation states have a degree of control over the extent to which inflation or deflation does operate within their frontiers.

Probably the world inflationary situation in the late 1960s and early 1970s was in part at least caused by the unwillingness or inability of the U.S. government to cure its balance-of-payments deficit. Be that as it may, it was still open to the British government to reduce the rise in prices. It is in this context that we will now examine some of the implications of inflation, the remedies available, and the effects which may be expected if inflation is allowed to continue at a high rate.

The *implications* have already been alluded to in earlier chapters, namely a redistribution of incomes in a politically or socially unacceptable manner. The refusal of successive governments to accept this redistribution and the use of fiscal methods, i.e. the tax system, to redress the situation may be politically praiseworthy, but at the same time keeps inflation alive in the sense that a new equilbrium based on real economic power within the community is constantly postponed.

So far as the *remedies* are concerned, it is of course always a good deal easier to define the problem and give the correct economic argument than to cure it in politically acceptable terms. Such remedies as there are, however, depend on an accurate analysis of what is meant by inflation.

It is convenient both in economic (and as we shall see in

political) terms to distinguish between two types of inflation, even though in real life they probably never have existed in isolation. These are (*a*) the conventional demand–pull inflation, the historical inflation as exemplified by the collapse of currencies after the First and Second World Wars, and (*b*) the relatively novel cost–push inflation.

Demand–pull inflation is almost literally too much money chasing too few goods. In this situation either the money supply has got completely out of control or goods for one reason or another are not available, indeed increasingly so, as the holders of goods of intrinsic value grow more and more unwilling to part with them for depreciating currency. The most spectacular example of this was Germany in the early 1920s when the currency collapsed, partly as a result of the reactions of the German government to French military pressure. Here money was rolling off the printing press to such an extent that it was literally so much paper. The same situation of a valueless currency occurred in Germany after the Second World War. Much less extreme examples of the situation have been seen in Britain during and immediately after the war when although the money supply was not out of control, consumer goods could not be produced in sufficient quantity to meet demand.

It is perhaps worth noting in passing that the present response to threatened inflation in Germany and elsewhere on the continent, which has gone through the process at its most extreme, is a good deal more severe than in the United Kingdom. One of the strongest weapons the monetary authorities have in these countries is an ingrained awareness of what happens to a society in this situation; the British public are probably a good deal more lethargic, because they have not passed through the traumatic experience of runaway inflation.

There are two ways of easing the situation if it threatens to get really out of control. First, if people really have lost confidence in a currency it will have to be replaced by a new currency which can somehow or another attract confidence. It may be necessary to go back to a currency which has an intrinsic value : gold for example – or more mundanely in the immediate post-war German scene cigarettes were an acceptable currency.

A less extreme alternative may be in effect to introduce a supplementary currency, through rationing, where ration books, points, etc., as well as the conventional currency are required. Of course, if rationing is pushed to the extreme, then the orthodox currency becomes in one sense almost superfluous; authorities introducing rationing generally make sure that certain commodities are available outside the rationing system, or permit or tolerate a 'free' market outside the system. Otherwise the original currency will simply cease to have relevance.

Rationing, of course, does not cure inflation, but it tends to suppress it in its most obvious forms and avoids some of the political consequences of a very rapid and very severe redistribution of income by ensuring the necessities of life to all.

The fact that, in spite of growing concern over inflation in the 1970s, few people have suggested rationing on wartime lines does suggest that, instinctively at least, people are aware that the inflation of the 1960s and 1970s is in some important respects different from the wartime situation. Thus increasing recognition has been given to another variety of inflation, the rather less well defined 'cost–push'.

Cost–push inflation has no readily acceptable definition because it is a political as much as an economic phenomenon. It is the situation where costs of production, particularly labour costs, are rising rapidly; it arises when sufficient trade unions achieve the means, or decide to enforce their power, to secure wage increases for their members which substantially exceed the growth in productivity and in the process create a spiral of rising expectations of further wage increases, rising costs and rising prices. Clearly, at this stage, action by a single trade union to improve or even simply to maintain its members' relative position worsens the spiral for all.

It had tended to be assumed for most of the post-war period that cost–push inflation was not likely to be a very serious proposition except in conditions of over-full employment. In this sense, referring back to the model of the first section, the assumption would be that the multiplier would, by successive increases in investment or any other injection (i.e., public expenditure or exports), push national income up in real terms to near full employment but that once that point was approached growth would be more and more in money terms and less and less in real terms.

The relative success in achieving very low unemployment without excessive inflation in the 1950s and early 1960s has been noted. But by the early 1970s, with unemployment at between 3 and 4 per cent, this earlier success had taken a knock. Obviously the reasons why growing unemployment did not stem cost–push inflation are debatable. It is at least arguable that the relationship still held, but at a lower rate, i.e. that cost inflation was still possible at say 5 per cent unemployment.

If this analysis is correct then the cure for cost inflation, assuming once again that it is not to be allowed to run its course, is economically simple but politically difficult. The economic remedy is for the government to be sufficiently ruthless to allow those companies which cannot compete to be put out of business even if this took the unemployment level to the point where it did pass whatever threshold existed, after which the inflationary spiral would be broken.

In terms of practical politics however this does not seem likely to happen. The 1970 Conservative government entered office, pledged to efficiency and the killing off of lame ducks. Whether it learned by experience, or simply lost its nerve when the confrontation came, is a matter of opinion. But by the end of 1972 it was clear that, like its predecessor, it would not allow a substantial portion of industry to sink, and this implicit life-belt probably played an important role in ensuring that wage demands in the affected industry were pitched with little regard to the costs involved.

If a ruthless sink-or-swim cure for cost inflation was no longer a political option then the alternative courses, within a free bargaining system, were somewhat limited and unspectacular. They consisted essentially of trying to break the spiral by persuasion and influence, encouraged by massive cuts in taxation to lower costs.

The basic problem is that there are economic solutions to inflation, but in a democratic society they may be politically unacceptable.

Demand–pull and Cost–push Inflation – How Valid is the Distinction?

It may have become apparent to the reader that whether we ascribe inflation to demand–pull or cost–push, the effects of rising prices and redistributing national income are much the same; although it may be helpful to identify the type of inflation so that different remedies can be tried, workable solutions that are politically acceptable are not all that more obvious.

The relationship between the two types of inflation is complex and imperfectly understood; any economic situation is likely to have elements of both and it is difficult to believe that they can be isolated and identified separately. In a sense, to paraphrase a fairly recent literary lioness, 'Inflation is inflation is inflation', and the distinction between the two forms may appear to be academic rather than politically realistic. It may well be, however, that this ability of governments to claim to identify an academic or even political distinction between two types of inflation gives, if not respectability, at least plausibility to a necessarily rather confused *mélange* of policies designed to cope with both recession and inflation.

The problem in a modern democratic society may be of inflationary pressures combined with insufficient effective demand for goods and services. The remedy for one of the two conditions is likely to worsen the other. Measures to deflate, cut wage settlements, increase taxation, and so on, may help to restrain inflation but at the expense of further adding to the deficit in overall demand for goods and services; conversely, trying to cure the demand deficit by making available more purchasing power worsens inflation. There is no way out of the dilemma, and a government has got to decide which of the two problems it regards as the more serious at any time and take the appropriate measures.

The distinction between demand–pull and cost–push inflation may give what is arguably a political justification for pursuing contradictory policies. If inflation can be labelled 'cost–push' then with a degree of plausibility, indeed logic, a government can simultaneously deflate in terms of opposing wage increases, while nevertheless reflating by increasing the money supply and purchasing power in general. The implicit assumption is being made that because inflation is not demand–pull, it will be possible to create increased demand without inflation.

The assumption is perhaps as dubious, but as politically convenient, as the idea that it is possible to have full, indeed overfull, employment without inflation being an ever-present threat. The truth is that however convenient it may be to distinguish between two types of inflation, the importance of the distinction is more in the room for manoeuvre and rationalisation of political decisions with inevitably messy consequences that it gives.

The Effects of Failure to Contain Inflation

Merely to look over Table 6 (p. 142) showing the overall fall in the value of money over the past fifty years or more is to reflect on failure. In a sense this is depressing but the fact that by and large the country has been able to withstand, or at least adjust to, changes in the value of money to the extent of a factor of six or seven during this time, does possibly suggest that the apocalyptic results threatened in much of what is written on the subject can be overdone.

It is fairly clear that successive governments in most western democracies have been prepared to tolerate, if indeed not to welcome, some inflation, say 2–3 per cent annually. Once it had become clear that full employment could not be taken for granted and that demand deficiency was a possibility, then governments were prepared to err on the side of slightly excessive demand rather than slightly deficient demand. Additionally of course, and less creditably, a slightly depreciated currency is a method of tacitly repudiating some of the burdens of debt.

A second point about the recurrent inflationary pressures is that there is no real evidence that inflation, provided it does not reach runaway proportions, is necessarily a check on real growth. This might seem an odd statement in view of Britain's relatively poor growth rate but an explanation is of course that inflationary pressures for most of the post-war years expressed themselves in the form of balance-of-payments crises, which had to be dealt with by credit squeezes earlier and more severely than would have been necessary if what had been at stake was an increase in inflation from say 3 per cent to 4 per cent.

Once the priorities had been changed, and sterling had been allowed to float, a crisis in 1972 which would have previously involved another 'stop–go' was not allowed to restrain continued real growth (or, unfortunately, inflation).

In hindsight it might well have been that in the first twenty-five years after the Second World War it would have been better to have gone for growth consistently. In that situation, the scenario would have been that balance-of-payments crises, when they came, would have been met less by credit squeezes or controls but by more frequent devaluations or simply by allowing the pound to float. Three consequences might have followed:

(*a*) Sterling's value would have fallen in the foreign exchange market even more than it has: £1 might have equalled $1 or even less.

(*b*) Inflation would have been a good deal worse than it has been, i.e. the internal value of the pound would have been much lower than it is.

(*c*) Finally if this condition of a depreciation of external value and internal inflation had been accepted, then in real terms the standard of living might have been higher than it is today, because it would have been clear that the priority was growth.

Whether, in hindsight, growth would have been as fast as, say, in France, which followed something like the above pattern, is of course arguable. Even if it were so, then whether this faster growth would have been a politically more acceptable policy is frankly impossible to say. The price for this growth would have been even more social conflict arising from the stresses of a generation of inflation than we have even today: and the ugly confrontations between trade unions and governments experienced occasionally in recent years might have been an everyday occurrence, as indeed they have been in societies which have been more willing to accept inflation.

It might seem quite pointless to speculate about the effects of opting for growth plus inflation a generation ago: it would be pointless but for one thing. It is important to realise that explicitly or implicitly a decision was made and renewed continuously over the years that, given a choice between growth on the one hand and with the accompanying disadvantages from the social and political point of view, and relative stability, political as well as economic, on the other, the choice was for the latter. Nevertheless it was a choice, and this problem of choice of priorities is one to which it will be necessary to return.

In this respect as in many other political and economic decisions there is on occasion a tendency to avoid contemplating the alternative in any detail. What happens if inflation is permitted over several years at a rate four or five times as great as the average since the war? It would be possible though not inevitable that real growth could be sustained. But what is more in doubt is whether a democratic and liberal government could survive the political and social pressures thus generated.

It is one of the ominous consequences that, sooner or later, economies which accept, or have to accept, this degree of inflation as a price of growth seem to end up authoritarian régimes whether of the Right or Left. Stable prices are not necessarily a prerequisite of economic growth – but they may be a prerequisite of a liberal democratic society.

CHAPTER 9

CHANGING PRIORITIES

THE previous chapters of this section listed and briefly examined five major objectives of any British government, namely,

rapid economic growth,

full employment,

a fair share-out of national income,

a reasonable economic balance among regions,

reasonably constant prices.

Had this book been written a few years ago, indeed any time up to the late 1960s, it would have been necessary to list another with a very high priority, namely a strong balance of payments. Almost overnight, however, it appears that this objective at least in its old form disappeared from the scene. Later in the chapter it will be useful to examine why this change took place but the fact that it occurred is a salutary lesson about any priority.

It has been noted that priorities can be rearranged and that if the economy fails to meet one or more of these objectives nothing very apocalyptic happens at least in the short run. The long-run consequences of failure can be inconvenient : indeed many of our political and economic problems in the 1970s stem from mediocre economic performance in the 1960s. It is therefore worth considering what will happen if the economy does fail to meet the objectives which are regarded as today's conventional wisdom; or indeed what will happen if we change the objectives.

There are two rather humbling truths on economic objectives which are only too easy to overlook.

The first of these is that more difficulties are self-suggested; more strictly perhaps that many of the constraints which exist in political or economic action in this country are self-imposed.

Secondly, virtually every one of the current economic objectives listed above has at one time or another been regarded as unattainable, irrelevant or unimportant. Looking briefly at each of these objectives :

(a) *Faster growth*. A good deal has been written here and

elsewhere about the relatively poor record of growth in the
United Kingdom in the post-war world compared with other
industrial countries. Two points can be made about this record :
first, the point which has already been commented on that even
the mediocre record of growth in the post-war years has been at
an unprecedented rate in historical terms. Growth in the century
and a half before probably averaged little more than 1 to 1.5 per
cent per annum, less than half of that of the post-war average.
Secondly, even at the beginning of the post-war period of growth
it was very far from clear that the, in hindsight, mediocre rate
actually achieved was even remotely possible. In so far as there
was any conscious thought about the situation in the period immediately after the end of the Second World War, a growth
rate of 1.5 per cent would have been regarded as very good. Much
of the post-war strategy was coloured by the supposition that another depression was possible after the post-war reconstruction
boom. Measurable G.D.P. figures were only laboriously being
compiled, and the scale of production potential was not clear.
It is easy to forget that the record which causes discontent today
would have seemed like unparalleled success a generation ago.
This is certainly not an argument for complacency. But getting
things into perspective, in spite of the undoubted desirability over
the next few years of achieving fast growth, it would be a mis-
take to imagine that inevitably the United Kingdom is committed
to fast growth for the indefinite future, even if this were to be
physically and financially possible.

(b) *Full employment* is likewise a relatively new concept, indeed a constantly evolving concept. Before the First World War
it was not really an issue – partly because mass unemployment
did not occur over long periods, partly because there was no
accurate statistical measure (some would say there is still no accurate statistical measure, though there are now published, and publicised, figures). Unemployment was not really recognised as an
issue until the 1920s and 1930s, because until then full employment was implicitly assumed to be normal. Certainly in so far as
full employment was seen as desirable and realisable, it was given
less priority than a strong currency. Even when the priorities
changed with the collapse of the gold standard system in 1931
the definition of full employment would probably have been
3 or 4 per cent unemployed. In the twenty years between the

wars unemployment averaged over 1 million and rose as high as 3 million on occasion, i.e. in double percentages.

Within the post-1945 period, definitions and expectations have changed. Full employment in the post-war planning phase was assumed to include about 3 per cent frictional unemployment. This figure, as has been remarked, was bettered in the next decade or two. By the early 1970s after six years of overall rise in unemployment, the definition of the acceptable level of unemployment was virtually impossible to establish; and it was likely to prove rather difficult to get back to the low figures of the 1950s and early 1960s.

Moreover, even when most committed to full employment and achieving a rate of round about 1 per cent unemployment, successive governments were ready in an emergency to switch priorities when sterling came under strain. The credit squeezes which were the consequence of sterling crises inevitably threatened a higher level of unemployment.

(c) *The fair share-out of national income.* It is more difficult to point to changes in attitudes towards the equitable distribution of income, because this is not easy to measure in the past. It is worth pointing out however that the so-called welfare state which is taken for granted today can be dated pretty precisely to 1948, when the Health Service in its present shape, as well as National Insurance and other forms of social security operated on a nation-wide basis for the first time. Hitherto, from about the beginning of the century, the boundary between state action to distribute national income, 'parish relief' and private charity has fluctuated, with the public sector commitment gaining overall. By the mid-1970s there were some political and economic arguments advanced in favour of 'negative income tax', i.e. a system whereby if an individual's income was below a certain minimum level, he would receive a payment from the tax authorities instead of paying them. If such a system were adopted the distinction between the tax and welfare systems would be even more eroded.

The other implication, namely that there may be a positive disincentive on the private individual to save for hard times or old age unless he can secure an income well above the minimum standard, is likely to be profound in the long run. Either the welfare state, which has progressively obscured the distinction between pensions based on earlier contributions and the previous public assistance, is likely to be altered; or some of the traditional virtues of thrift are going to be regarded as irrelevant, indeed harmful to an individual's interests.

(*d*) *A reasonable balance among regions.* Regional policy, even after forty years, is in a sense in its infancy. Certainly there is little evidence of consistency over this period, let alone substantial success. A very significant technological factor in recent years is that modern industry is fairly footloose, unlike traditional industry whose location was determined by the geographical proximity of raw materials, iron or coal deposits, or at the very least by access to bulk supplies of raw materials from overseas. Most modern industries rely on relatively small amounts of raw materials, compared with the technology involved, and are able to use energy from a national grid or piped in liquid or gas form at little running expense. There is little obvious advantage in one site as against another in national terms, and it is only because of this that there is any option about regional development.

(*e*) *Reasonably constant prices.* As has already emerged there have been times when falling, rather than rising, prices were the problem. Indeed that particular problem was so acute in the United States in the 1930s that President Roosevelt raised the price of gold in an attempt to stimulate a recovery in demand by raising the overall level of prices.

As has been pointed out, it is by no means certain that the problem of inflation will be a persistent one. Even if it is however the problem can be lived with. The psychological and political problems created by inflation are in some respects more important than the economic ones. The main fear is the subconscious assumption that the end result could be the complete collapse of a currency like the German Mark in the 1920s. Such a catastrophic situation is not impossible; it is however extremely unlikely.

The fact is of course that a British government faced with either growth or inflation has a choice. The indications are that in the 1970s the choice is for growth and the political price of stopping inflation – perhaps with up to 10 per cent unemployment – is regarded in present conditions as politically unacceptable.

This opting for growth at a steady high level regardless of the fallout elsewhere is a significant change of priorities in the past few years. One result of this reversal of priorities is that the international role of sterling has been sacrificed, a point which will be discussed next. If the present attempts to control inflation fail, as the international role of sterling failed, the reversal of traditional attitudes, already obvious, could become more dramatic.

In other words it is quite possible, even if highly undesirable, to drop this objective, possibly settling for a steady rise in prices without too much fluctuation. If a government is prepared to pay the political price, i.e. the redistribution of national income, then constant prices, as an aim, could go into limbo as dramatically as the external role of sterling.

A Deposed Objective – A Strong Balance of Payments

In the past few years there has been a dramatic turn round in policy and priorities. After a quarter of a century of the post-war world the objective of a strong balance of payments has apparently receded as a primary if not the primary objective of British policy.

Why was a strong balance of payments so important, and why was it apparently possible to downgrade its priority virtually overnight?

The basic reason for a strong balance of payments was to maintain sterling as a key international currency, which other nations would hold as reserves, and which would be used extensively as a trading currency. Sterling was, before the First World War, virtually the only international currency, more convenient even than gold. Two world wars and the intervening financial crises had effectively destroyed sterling's claim to be *the* world's currency. But from the wreckage of the pre-war gold standard and the financial chaos of the inter-war years the Sterling Area had emerged. An exact definition of what was meant by the Sterling Area is difficult. It meant different things at different times, but in essence it was a group of countries, mainly Commonwealth, who held their reserves in sterling rather than gold or dollars, and added to or drew out of the Bank of England central reserves of gold and hard currencies, as and when appropriate. The gold and currency reserves of the United Kingdom were in the last analysis the reserves for the entire monetary area.

Apart from the political advantages of being the centre of an international monetary system the United Kingdom's role as a

world banker had certain economic advantages and disadvantages – with, as it turned out, the disadvantages predominating.
But before the failure of the system became clear, for the quarter
of a century following the end of the Second World War, the
defence of the Sterling Area system was a first priority.

The main financial and economic advantage was that a great
deal of the wartime debts accumulated by the United Kingdom
were transferred into currency backing and reserves by other member nations and did not immediately represent a realised claim
on the inadequate resources of the U.K. economy in the post-war
years. Indeed, instead of trying to repay these wartime debts, the
U.K. government encouraged overseas investment by British
companies replacing assets overseas which had had to be sold
during or immediately after the Second World War. Over some
twenty years the overseas assets of U.K. companies grew immensely, far exceeding those sold as a consequence of the
war.

The disadvantages were formidable, however. Although the
ratio of assets to liabilities was reasonable, indeed favourable,
most of the U.K. overseas assets were in the form of long-term
investments while the liabilities were to a large extent short-term.
In fact the ratio of short-term assets to liabilities was only about
one in four.

The result was that whenever there was a run on sterling occasioned by poor balance-of-trade figures, a situation developed
where there was every incentive to speculate on the possible devaluation of sterling. During the late 1940s and throughout the
1950s there was almost a two-yearly cycle of such crises – 1947,
1949, 1951, 1955, 1957, 1959 – and on every occasion the price
of defending sterling was a credit squeeze, a slashing back of
investment at home and a consequent check on growth. The
'stop–go' which was so characteristic of the growth pattern of this
period was the direct result; in the long run, however, it was not
merely the periods of very slow growth which occurred so much
as the uncertainty generated which proved disastrous. Businessmen simply could not rely on two or three years of uninterrupted
growth when planning future investment.

The fallout from the priority given to the balance-of-payments
question was not all untoward however. At least the inflationary
situation was kept under control on two accounts. First, an ad-

verse balance of trade, i.e. a surplus of imports, was a form of leakage of purchasing power as defined in the first section, and this potentially meant a smaller multiplier effect and less inflation. Secondly, actions to correct the balance-of-payments crises, such as a credit squeeze which was intended to reinforce the external value of sterling, could not but strengthen the internal value as well.

It would be tedious to follow out the course of events on the balance-of-payments front during this long post-war spell, beyond making the point that governments, Labour and Conservative, put the defence of sterling as a very high priority: not, to be strictly accurate, as the first priority as it seems to have been in the 1920s, but high up the list, and indeed when sterling crises occurred the defence did get first priority, over full employment.

There were several Pyrrhic victories and two lost battles in the struggle. One of these, the forced devaluation of 1949, shook the Sterling Area, but in so far as the great majority of Sterling Area members followed Britain's example and devalued too, the system survived. The system began to erode in the 1950s as more and more freedom of action was sought by member nations, mainly for the right to hold a proportion of their reserves in other currencies than sterling, or to get guarantees against further devaluation. There were, however, no dramatic crises precisely because the whole system was a pragmatic one, constantly evolving and therefore affording few significant breaches of principle which would mark an end to the system.

The running crisis of 1964–7 effectively finished sterling as a major reserve currency though the death certificate was not issued until the early 1970s. In 1967, after three years' intermittent crisis, massive borrowings and slow growth, sterling had to be devalued in almost the worst possible circumstances. The variation in response of other Sterling Area members, some of which devalued while others did not, signalled the progressive breaking up of the cohesiveness of the system. That the system limped on after 1967 arose largely from the fact that there was no obvious alternative reserve currency for former members to hold instead of sterling – the obvious rival, the dollar, also being in difficulties.

If the other members of the Sterling Area were showing an increasing reluctance to accept the disciplines of the system, the attitude of the British Labour government and the Conservative

Opposition was undergoing a reluctant transformation, and that for both internal domestic and external political reasons.

In the first instance years of relatively slow growth and sacrifice had in the event been wasted – and British politicians might have wondered whether the game was worth the candle, particularly in the light of disillusion about the worth of the Commonwealth concept. Secondly, and of growing importance, was the impatience of the United Kingdom's prospective partners in the Common Market, particularly the French. There were important political issues at stake, but the main economic argument was the continental attitude that British unwillingness to cure the chronic sickness of sterling in an acceptable manner was resulting in British inflationary pressures being exported to the rest of the world. Thus, in so far as British freedom of action was limited by the requirements of being the central banker for the Sterling Area, this was a stumbling block to U.K. membership of the European Economic Community.

In the event it was the Conservative government elected in 1970 which made the sacrifice, if it was really a sacrifice, by agreeing to pay off gradually the sterling balances of other members of the area. The logic of this was that Britain was no longer acting as a central banker for a monetary area which was being wound up over the years. The final symbolic act however came in mid-1972 when yet another sterling crisis blew up. This time instead of defending sterling by the traditional method of a credit squeeze which might have bought relief by stopping growth, the government in very short order decided not to reverse its policies but to go for continued growth. Sterling was left to find its own value instead of being defended at the then prevailing rate of $2.60 – it was allowed to float.

This was a solution which in a sense had always been there – provided the implications were accepted. The fact that the choice had not been made before was perhaps an instance of the type of self-imposed restraint on action mentioned earlier. Admittedly the option had been brought to the fore by the American example in 1971 when for a time the dollar was allowed to float. Nevertheless the action of the British government was a remarkable reversal of the priorities of the past twenty-five years. In a sense with the abdication of responsibility for the Sterling Area system and the downgrading of the importance of a strong balance of payments as a necessary prerequisite, a major preoccupation disappeared, virtually painlessly overnight, simply because the government had jettisoned one of its priorities.

It is of course easy to say in hindsight that this should have been done years before, or that the previous sterling crises had thereby demonstrably been self-induced. There is a good case for so arguing; but the argument can be carried dangerously far in so far as it assumes that somehow floating a currency is a gimmick which has no ill effects. There were certainly side effects, some of which would take years to show through. Not least the anti-inflationary discipline of the old priority of fixed exchange rates was badly missed. Even if the continental powers had less justi-fication for a complaint that inflation was being exported, the pressures of inflation were built up further in the British economy already under pressure : the lower the exchange rate sank the greater was the internal inflationary effect.

Conclusion. The point of the last few pages has been to illus-trate what is so frequently forgotten, namely that few priorities are immutable, and in that sense many of our present problems are, if not self-suggested, at least self-imposed for political reasons which may not stand the test of time.

It has to be recognised that priorities can and do change; that our perception of what is right and important in economic and political terms may change from generation to generation, or even from decade to decade. The true art of the politician in economic affairs may be to sense, well before the economists or the civil servants, when society wishes to change its priorities, and ease the way for these changes. Arguably, many economic problems in modern western society are not really solved; they may go away in the sense that they are no longer seen as important. It would be a bold man who would claim that our present priorities, as listed earlier, will continue to loom as large or in the same order in Britain in the 1980s or 1990s.

Lastly, in a discussion about priorities, particularly deposed priorities, it is only too easy to see developments as the gradual recognition that certain restraints or priorities are self-imposed and that therefore they ought to be dispensed with. But if a prior-ity can be deposed as the economic or political climate changes, it can equally well be reinstated. It may well be, for example, that after a year or two of the practical disadvantages of virtually ignoring the balance-of-payments issue, or the full employment issue, these will be restored to their former importance at the expense of the current front runners. What we are observing is not necessarily a gradual stripping away of the inessential priorities in favour of the eternally valid, but a situation where virtually any economic priority can only be judged relative to the other economic, political or moral priorities preoccupying society at any one time.

An Undeclared Objective

In the last few chapters we have discussed those objectives, not always compatible with each other, which would receive general support from the majority of the electorate and which in this sense have to jostle for priority.

Most or all of these objectives are only in part economic, and there are, of course, many other purely political or even moral objectives which a government may choose to pursue : few if any of these will be without their economic consequences. But there is one objective of any government which will affect economic policy in a democratic society, and that is the determination of the party in power to win the next general election : and the nearer one is to a general election, the more important does this factor become.

This is an observation which might seem to be either cynical or trite. In a sense both charges are true. But so far as the charge of cynicism is concerned, any politician of conviction is likely to act on the assumption that what is good for his party is good for the country. In that sense the aim of perpetuating his party in office at times becomes a legitimate, even a praiseworthy, aim of economic policy. As to the charge of triteness, the general election factor becomes not only important, but to some extent realisable, in the nature and timing of economic decisions. Few governments have a death wish, even in the most adverse economic circumstances.

It is therefore one of the political facts of life that governments today have an element of control over economic events and their timing. They can, to an extent, shuffle priorities and time economic decisions to achieve results, not *sub specie aeternitatis* but with an eye to the next election or more strictly the year running up to the election. On occasion the timing of the next election

F

can be more important than the economic facts of the situation.

There are some conventional received truths about economic conditions and their effects on elections. Examples which probably figure prominently in current calculations are

that high unemployment loses an election,

that rising unemployment loses an election,

that rising prices lose an election.

In passing, received truths explain how to lose elections : there are no sovereign remedies to win them.

A problem about received truths is that either they can be proved wrong in the event, or at least they are not eternal. One exploded received truth mentioned earlier was the conviction in the 1950s that a credit squeeze severe enough to push unemployment up to say half a million would lose an election. Such a credit squeeze, heralded by an unparalleled 7 per cent bank rate, was introduced by the Conservatives in 1957 in the balance-of-payments crisis of that year. It was seen then as an act of daring or desperation, according to one's political viewpoint. In the event the government won the next election handsomely and that particular received truth went into limbo.

Nevertheless few governments challenge received truths if they can avoid it, especially as an election draws near. Moreover if we accept that most measures affecting investment or employment take between one and two years to have a marked effect on the economy, it is apparent that political factors become increasingly important after say the halfway mark between elections.

There is only limited room for manoeuvre. Thus there may be very obvious constraints : bottlenecks in the economy; external economic or political effects beyond the influence of the governments; or simply earlier policies which have gone wrong or are taking too long to mature and have to be modified or scrapped in a hurry. But, given these real-life restraints, some economic planning may implicitly depend as much on when the results are required to be acceptable to or welcomed by the general public as on their economic efficiency or even doctrinal purity.

Understandably there is a limit on what can be done not only economically, but politically. The general public can be both cynical and idealistic : cynical, in the sense that a too overtly well-timed economic boom at election time is as likely to lose votes as win them; idealistic, in the sense that they will respect tough and theoretically unpopular decisions if they are convinced that the government is competent and acting in the best long-term interests of the community. It would be dangerous therefore to assume that governments are always successful in their efforts to create politically popular economic situations in the months before a general election, or that the general public necessarily responds in gratitude. Nevertheless it would be naive to ignore the fact that it is possible to influence events and, in a rough-and-ready way, time the impact of politically popular or unpopular measures. Political timing of this sort is a factor acknowledged or unacknowledged in political situations.

Additionally when, as in the United Kingdom, the government has considerable discretion as to when it actually holds the election, this freedom of manoeuvre is considerable and the advantage to the government in power substantial. If it gets its timing of economic events slightly wrong, it can change the timetable.

In a pragmatic society like the United Kingdom no government, short of absolute economic incompetence, is likely to lose an election on its economic performance alone. It is standard political tactics for an Opposition to demand an election when unpopular economic measures are in operation, claiming that the government has no mandate for its action : a charge which is, of course, virtuously refuted by the government. The corollary is that when a government does call an election before it is compelled to do so, the Opposition then charges it with going to the country prematurely because it wants to get the election over before the economic disasters which loom ahead strike.

The charge and counter-charge are treated with a certain degree of cynicism by both politicians and public. But beneath the political comedy there is a serious economic and political truth, that economic policy can be subordinated to electoral timetables; and the more accurate the knowledge of the demand effects and time lags of changes of economic policy becomes, the more important does the political timing of decisions become.

CHAPTER 10

A CASE STUDY IN CHANGING PRIORITIES 1970–4

THE last chapter in Part I attempted to compare economic theory with political reality by discussing some events of recent years in terms of the concepts outlined in Chapters 1 and 2. This, the last chapter of Part II, has a rather similar aim, namely to compare the desirable objectives outlined in the previous chapters with what has actually been achieved, and in particular how the priorities were changed from time to time.

The period from mid-1970 to early 1974 covers the accession to power of the new Heath government, the entry of the United Kingdom into the European Economic Community and the dramatic rise in oil prices, which marked the end of an era of cheap power. It was a traumatic period in more senses than one. At one level it can be seen as a period when many cherished Conservative ideas were dropped, and many words were eaten or choked upon – an example of political pragmatism or lack of principle depending on the reader's political convictions. In a deeper sense what was taking place was a fumbling with, then a reassessment of, economic priorities and the means to achieve them. It is in this context that the events will be examined, not as a case for or against what the Conservatives said out of office and did in office.

The previous chapters examined objectives which had widespread, indeed non-party support, in terms of growth, full employment, etc. To these must be added, tentatively, a strong balance of payments. In June 1970 this priority had not been decisively rejected, and for most of the previous twenty-five years had been at or near the top of the priorities.

But if these were generally acceptable 'non-party' objectives, were there any specifically Conservative objectives which had, for example, featured in the election campaign? There were at least four which were significant enough to affect the other non-party ones. These can be summarised :

That taxation was too high and ought to be reduced. How this objective would affect the distribution of national income depended on the type of tax cuts envisaged. Broadly, however, cuts in direct taxation, i.e. income and surtax or corporation tax would benefit the better off, particularly if they shifted the emphasis on to indirect taxation, i.e. consumption.

The obverse of this objective was a second, namely *that public expenditure ought to be cut*, i.e. not only did heavy public expenditure force up taxation but it was potentially inflationary. Again the effects on the distribution of national income depended on what sort of expenditure was cut. If cuts were in the social security field, for example, the results would be regressive rather than progressive.

That the genuinely less well-off sectors of the community ought to be protected. The idea that a Right-wing, fairly hard line, government was concerned to protect the poorer sections of the community was received with well-publicised scepticism by the new government's political opponents. But in so far as the Conservatives saw a major source of hardship among the poor, particularly the pensioners, as arising in part from the ability of the powerful, including the trade unions, to obtain more than a fair share of national wealth, there was nothing particularly 'unconservative' in this policy.

The long-term *simplification and reform of a tax system* (and perhaps a social security system) which had been a major theme of conservative thinking while in Opposition.

How far these four additional aims could be achieved individually or collectively depended on a number of imponderables, not least the ability to create more disposable wealth for the whole community by achieving rapid growth, the first of the non-party objectives; and on a more personal level on the ability of the new Prime Minister and Chancellor of the Exchequer to push their declared aims through. Incidentally, one of the first reverses of the new government was the death of the Chancellor Mr Macleod who had just come into office with the reputation of a reforming Chancellor.

It might be argued that there was an objective which overrode all the others in the mind of the new Prime Minister, namely to negotiate membership of the Common Market. In a sense however this was a vital but essentially political objective which pervaded all the others, including the economic ones.

Common Market membership could not affect any short-term measures to deal with the economic situation. Such measures could not wait, particularly since membership could not be assumed in June 1970. Moreover any long-term measures implicit in Common Market membership, e.g. the introduction of a value added tax system, were seen as desirable in themselves regardless of the outcome of the negotiations.

The Economic Indicators

Any government, at any time, has a series of economic indicators – statistics either collected specifically or, as has been remarked, as a by-product of the routine working of the economy. These economic indicators give a measure of how well, or how badly, the economy is performing. Some of these are confidential, others are highly technical and beyond the scope of this book. But of the published indicators, some five or six published monthly in practice yield most of the available information. Those which will be used in this chapter are the following.

The Index of Industrial Production is an obvious candidate for inclusion on the list. Its main advantage is that it is calculated monthly, albeit with a two-month delay, and is therefore more speedily available than estimates in changes of national product which can be made only at quarterly intervals, and then after two or three months' delay. Nevertheless the Index of Industrial Production has in practice some limitations as an indicator of what is happening in the national economy. In the first instance it covers only industry and not the other activities which constitute a large part of national economic activity. Moreover like any other indicator which has to be produced fairly quickly if it is to be of more than historic interest it is liable to be revised and corrected during the next two or three months after its initial publication. The reason for this is that the Index is based only on a sample of industrial activity: the information, given essentially on a voluntary basis, is not always available on time in a form appropriate for monthly treatment and with a sufficient degree of acceptability. While therefore the Central Statistical Office is constantly attempting to improve the sample and refine the results, the level of accuracy can never be guaranteed absolutely. One or two per cent annual growth is likely to show up on a monthly basis as a fraction of one per cent, at times smaller than the possible error, or the subsequent revision. The figures shown below are rounded off to the nearest whole number.

The monthly count of *registered unemployed*. Some of the alternatives have been discussed earlier in Chapter 5 and will not be reviewed here. Two series will be shown, the seasonally adjusted figure for Great Britain and unadjusted figures for the United Kingdom. In view of the political situation in Northern Ireland it is arguable that that province cannot be regarded as reflecting economic conditions elsewhere : moreover in economic strategy it is the long-term trend without seasonal peaks and troughs that matter. In political terms however the situation is not that simple. The largest seasonally unadjusted U.K. figures get the publicity, especially if a key figure like one million unemployed is reached; and government policy may be affected by public reaction to the unadjusted U.K. figures as well as by the more meaningful seasonally adjusted figure.

The final indicator with which we are concerned is the *visible balance of trade*. This is by no means the only balance-of-payments figure which matters, but gives a quick indicator about how far the United Kingdom is paying her way in the world. To each month's figure for the visible balance can be added £50 million or more, the average surplus on invisibles, i.e. the surplus on banking, insurance, shipping, tourism, etc. Roughly then, if the balance of trade is not more than about £60 millions in the red the situation is satisfactory. There is one very important qualification however. The figure published monthly is seasonally adjusted; the actual total of receipts and payments in any one month is not now published. This is understandable, since a month's figures may be almost meaningless. But the fact that the Department of Trade and Industry does not feel obliged to publish crude figures, unlike the Department of Employment on registered unemployment figures, has two results of political significance. First, the importance of temporary fluctuations is played down and this probably reduces speculation as a result; less desirably the seasonally adjusted figures (discreetly corrected over the next month or two) may delay recognition of a change in the trend for better or worse for a month or two.

These then are the figures shown in the remainder of the chapter. The reader should bear in mind three points. At any one time the figures published are a few weeks or months out of date;

and they may be only approximate, subject to later correction. The figures shown below are, by and large, those available at the time to the government – supplemented of course by the confidential or more complex indicators mentioned earlier. Finally the bases on which figures are compiled are subject to change of definition from time to time. Some of the series therefore are not strictly comparable throughout the whole period under discussion. This point however has largely been ignored and no attempt has been made to explain the changes in detail or revise the earlier figures retrospectively. What mattered was what the figures indicated *at the time they were available*, regardless of whether they were later shown to be right or wrong. Where figures were significantly revised the revised figures are shown only at the point they became available : thus when the same month's figures are quoted more than once, a different value may appear.

The Situation in June 1970

When the Heath government was returned to power in June 1970 it faced fewer external constraints on its freedom of manoeuvre than any previous post-war government.

So far as economic growth was concerned the past record was relatively poor but the potential growth prospects were brighter. Thus the G.D.P. growth record during the previous government's term of office had followed a striking pattern.

TABLE 7

PERCENTAGE GROWTH IN REAL G.D.P.
OVER PREVIOUS YEAR

1964	5·7
1965	2·9
1966	1·8
1967	1·6
1968	3·6
1969	2·0

In the previous five years only one year had shown growth at about the productive potential of 3–3.5 per cent. The relatively slow growth from 1965 onwards had been caused by successive credit squeezes, and their effects on business confidence. Initially these credit squeezes had been the classic answer to a chronic balance-of-payments deficit inherited in this instance from the previous Conservative government in 1964. Ironically, although the credit squeeze failed in its objective of saving the exchange rate of sterling, it still had to be reimposed after the November 1967 devaluation to ensure that devaluation did indeed work on this occasion. But whatever might be said about the price in growth terms, the devaluation appeared to have succeeded by 1969 when the United Kingdom went into surplus on the current account.

The last Labour government Budget had been introduced in 1970 against this background, i.e. it was expansionary in intent; it was calculated at the time that the measures taken would produce a 3.5 per cent growth up to mid-1971 at about the same rate as the growth productive capacity. By implication therefore the last Labour Budget would not add substantially to inflationary pressures; nor would it cut unemployment by very much.

Thus if the Labour Chancellor, Mr Jenkins (and his official advisers), were correct, and the Conservatives let things be, a reasonable rate of growth would be achieved in their first year of office.

The major questions were: was the forecast of 3.5 per cent growth correct? And, if it was, would the Conservatives accept the priorities established by the previous government?

The answer to the first question was that only time would tell; the answer to the second was, in the short run yes, in the long run probably not.

How did the available indicators stand about June 1970? (See Table 8, p. 170.)

The expected growth (as indicated in the Index of Industrial Production) had yet to materialise; this, however, was not conclusive evidence that the policy of expansion was not working since the March 1970 measures had not yet had time to work through.

The columns which were likely to cause the most immediate concern were those on prices and unemployment. On the *price* side, quite apart from the dismal picture shown by the Index, there were ominous signs in rising earnings. These were far ahead of any likely expansion of production; well ahead indeed of any expected growth in G.D.P. or productivity per head. Thus in June 1970 the indications were that earnings were up by about

TABLE 8

	Industrial production (1963=100)	Retail prices Jan 1962=100	Annual % increase	Registered unemployed G.B. (s.a.)	U.K. (unadjusted) Thousands	Balance of trade (s.a.) £ millions
1964	111	107·0	3·3	381	413	−395
1965	114	112·1	4·8	329	360	− 77
1966	115	116·5	3·9	360	391	+ 43
1967	117	119·4	2·5	560	599	−312
1968	125	125·0	4·7	564	601	−319
1969	123	131·8	5·4	560	597	+414
1970						
Jan	123	135·5	5·0	530	667	+ 38
Feb	124	136·2	4·9	557	661	− 7
Mar	126	137·0	5·1	567	660	+ 5
Apr	125	139·1	5·6	567	652	− 10
May	122	139·5	6·1	560	612	− 32

11 to 12 per cent on 12 months previously, and showed signs of rising faster.

The unemployment figures could be read in two ways. The seasonally adjusted figure suggested that the situation was unsatisfactory, but not necessarily getting worse : the unadjusted figures were falling during the summer and public concern presumably was not too great.

Given that action to reduce rising prices would possibly raise the unemployment rate, and that action to cut unemployment would adversely affect prices, which way was the government to act?

The fact that inflation was running at about as high a rate as ever recorded in peacetime was particularly significant, not least in the light of a widely quoted (and no doubt subsequently regretted) election undertaking by Mr Heath to reduce the rise in prices 'at a stroke'.

Before considering what happened when this priority was translated into action the other economic indicator on the balance of trade was fairly satisfactory. The initial reaction of the Conservative Opposition to the November 1967 devaluation was highly critical : this criticism had been muted when the overall pattern began to come right in 1969 and early in 1970. The last few months however were less satisfactory, and might indeed

be read by a pessimist as signalling a return to deficit: the recent
trend had certainly not helped Labour in the election campaign;
but allowing for the surplus on invisibles of about £50 millions
monthly, the current balance was still 'in the black'. Although
part of this good showing could only be attributed to the amount
of slack in the economy, the inference was that, short of a disastrous worsening in the next few months, the current balance was
not likely to be a serious constraint on growth, particularly since
the capital account was looking healthy.

The government made no significant change in its first four
months of office. The instinct to 'wait and see' was probably
reinforced by the unexpected death of the Chancellor, Mr Macleod, regarded as one of the major assets of the new government.
His successor, Mr Barber, was in the event to prove one of the
strongest reforming Chancellors of the century. This, however,
was not immediately apparent at the time.

By the time of the new Chancellor's first serious review of the
economic situation, in Parliament, a few more indicators were
available. The picture was now as in Table 9.

TABLE 9

	Industrial production	Retail prices	Annual % increase	Registered unemployed G.B. (s.a.) U.K. (unadjusted) Thousands		Balance of trade (s.a.) £ millions
1970						
Jan	123	135·5	5·0	530	667	+ 38
Feb	124	136·2	4·9	557	661	− 7
Mar	126	137·0	5·1	567	660	+ 5
Apr	125	139·1	5·6	567	652	− 10
May	122	139·5	6·1	560	612	− 32
June	123	139·9	5·9	561	579	− 48
July	122	140·9	6·7	593	608	+131
Aug	123	140·8	6·8	593	645	−231
Sep	125	141·5	7·0	589	666	+ 5

Such information as there was suggested that while growth
had yet to materialise, unemployment was if anything slightly
worsening, but that inflation was visibly accelerating. The
balance-of-trade figures suggested that, given the monthly £50
million surplus on the invisibles, the outlook was reasonable in

spite of temporary distortions in June and July, caused by a dock strike.

Possibly as a result of the uncertain trends the Chancellor's October statement indicated few real changes in the inherited priorities: so far as the specifically Conservative priorities were concerned the statement contained an undertaking to cut tax, particularly income tax, in the next Budget, together with corresponding cuts in public expenditure. Some social security changes were raised, but provision was made for the less well-off families.

In regional policy investment grants were to be phased out, followed in four years' time by the regional employment premium, making way for tax incentives which would favour the profitable firms in the regions. These changes were foreshadowed in the pre-election pledges, and apart from a mild boost did nothing significantly to alter the growth forecast of 3.5 per cent set by the last Labour Chancellor.

There was still no very clear indication as yet on whether inflation or unemployment was the worst evil, but the Chancellor was no doubt already giving serious thought on how his priorities would be arranged in the March 1971 Budget, the first Conservative Budget since the election.

The figures in Table 10 show how the situation developed during the winter of 1970–1 and the known situation at the time of the Budget.

TABLE 10

	Industrial production	Retail prices	Annual % increase	Registered unemployed G.B. (s.a.) U.K. (unadjusted) Thousands		Balance of trade (s.a.) £ millions
1970						
Sep	126	141·5	7·0	589	666	+19
Oct	125	143·0	7·4	576	634	+42
Nov	123	144·0	7·9	579	639	+56
Dec	125	145·0	7·9	589	658	−11
1971						
Jan	127	147·0	8·5	614	731	−11
Feb	124	147·8	8·5	623	761	−63

By now however more accurate G.D.P. figures were becoming

available for most of 1970, by which the 3.5 per cent growth target could be checked. It was by now apparent that the target was not at all likely to be achieved.

Why had the forecasts gone wrong, as so often in the past?

In the first instance the March 1970 estimate of the then current rate of growth had proved to be over-optimistic. And from this lower than expected starting-off point there was additionally a less than expected growth in demand. The situation was perhaps a classic example of the difference between an economic model, where at any time the economic situation and a set rate of growth could be taken as already known, and a real-life situation where information is rather less conveniently to hand.

Quite *why*, in the real-life situation, the growth in demand and therefore output had lagged is debatable. Undoubtedly however a major factor was the state of business opinion, where morale was low after the experiences of the previous few years. Businessmen were not necessarily reacting in a rational economic way, but instinctively, from a mood of doubt and uncertainty. Economic forecasts were therefore not telling the full story.

In the circumstances it was not very surprising that unemployment was still rising, as the gap between actual output growth and productive capacity growth remain unclosed. But of more immediate concern to the Chancellor was the acceleration in the rate of inflation, not only in the Retail Price Index shown, but also in the rising figure for earnings – now about 14 per cent up on the previous year.

The need to fight inflation was illustrated by serious reversals in the policy of discouraging substantial pay settlements. Local government manual workers and electricity supply workers won substantial increases. A postal workers' strike was more successfully resisted; but the 7 per cent settlement was hardly a decisive victory for moderating wage claims.

The March 1971 Budget

Tax cuts, direct and indirect, were fairly generous – in round figures nearly £50 millions in the 1971–2 financial year. Pensions were increased by 20 per cent, but most of the increased cost was to be met from increased contributions.

At first glance the Budget looked like a substantial cut in taxation and therefore a boost in demand over the previous year;

in view of the existing spare capacity this might have been expected to produce rapid growth. But the truth was rather more complex than the simple tax cuts suggested. The most important factor was the rate of inflation over the past year, and the phenomenon of fiscal drag, i.e. because rapid inflation had caused a rapid rise in *money* incomes, there had been a more than proportional rise in tax revenues. Thus, much of the tax cuts merely restored the March 1970 tax ratios in *real* terms. Moreover the changes in social security rates and benefits complicated the picture; higher contributions were virtually an increase in taxation on the better-off section of the community, and an increase in transfer incomes to the worse-off, i.e. the pensioners. Since pensioners have a higher marginal propensity to consume than the community as a whole (that is they find it more difficult to save anything), the effect was slightly to increase demand. But the overall effect nevertheless was largely to keep the pressure of demand as before, with growth likely at 3 per cent, i.e. at slightly below productive potential.

Why did the Chancellor not go for faster growth which was obviously possible given the gap between output and productive potential?

One must assume that what was involved was the conflict of priorities between unemployment and inflation. By implication inflation was at this time, and on the evidence available, regarded as the more serious situation, and the government therefore was prepared to delay faster growth while inflation was being contained.

That was the priority at the time of the Budget. Within four months however the priorities had changed. In July a fresh set of measures were added to the March Budget, in effect if not in name, a supplementary Budget.

The indicators in Table 11 (p. 175) tell part of the story.

The July 1971 Measures

Once again taxes were cut, particularly on the consumer side; cuts in purchase tax were accompanied by the abolition of hire-purchase controls. If past experience were anything to go by such measures would cause a rapid build-up of demand on the consumer side and, it was to be hoped, on output.

On the capital side too there were generous tax allowances on

TABLE 11

	Industrial production	Retail prices	Annual % increase	Registered unemployed		Balance of trade (s.a.) £ millions
				G.B. (s.a.)	U.K. (unadjusted)	
				Thousands		
1971						
Jan	127	147·0	8·5	614	731	− 12
Feb	124	147·8	8·5	623	761	− 66
Mar	123	149·0	8·8	657	793	0
Apr	126	152·2	9·4	704	814	+ 16
May	126	153·2	9·8	731	794	+ 28

new plant and machinery expenditure over the next two years, with further concessions to the development regions.

Taken with the March measures taxation had been cut by about £1100 millions in the 1971–2 financial year. This was tax cutting on a spectacular scale, and incidentally a fulfilling of one of the specifically Conservative objectives.

But the main purpose of the measures lay in the attempt to stimulate rapid and short-term expansion, mainly on the consumer side (*C* in the original model). Rapid expansion was now the order of the day.

But why had the priorities been rearranged in such a short time?

In introducing the measures, the Chancellor revealed that the estimates of output on which he had based his Budget statement had turned out to be optimistic. This was the second year in succession in which this had happened, and is perhaps yet again an example of how difficult it is in a modern dynamic economy to know exactly what is happening in time to make significant changes.

Because of this error in estimating output at the time of the Budget the 3 per cent growth target by mid-1972 would almost certainly not be reached on the basis merely of the Budget measures. The new measures however would take output up to 4–4.5 per cent by mid-1972, from the lower base.

There were two important changes in policy implicit in this change. The 4–4.5 per cent growth planned would take output over the growth of productive capacity in the same period, and would presumably take up some of the slack in the economy. It would thus, fairly rapidly, cut unemployment even if it did nothing to contain inflation. Clearly, since March, inflation had been replaced by unemployment as the major evil. Why had the priorities changed so quickly?

There had been no improvement in the inflationary situation. Indeed the situation had got worse but more important were the indications that unemployment was rising more rapidly than ever.

But if growth, and particularly a cut in the unemployment figures, were the first priority, the control of inflation still came a close second. The main measure in this field was an initiative from the Confederation of British Industries to persuade their members to hold down price rises to not more than 5 per cent in the following year. The measure was widely supported by the C.B.I. membership, largely because of its shrewd timing. The restraint was reinforced by the adherence to the 5 per cent maximum by the nationalised industries, no doubt under some pressure from the government which would have to foot the bill for any deficits thus incurred. A somewhat sanguine hope was expressed by the adherents to the restraint that the trade unions would follow their example in moderation.

The potential contradictions between measures to stimulate demand and measures to restrain inflation were now illustrated by the steady growth in money supply. The Bank of England by this means was making it very easy for an industrialist contemplating investment to borrow money.

The argument about whether this rapid growth in money supply was inflationary has already been discussed in Chapter 8. It can be said that there were outside critics who disputed the view that this increase was not particularly inflationary: at the very least, the additional money supply and cuts in interest rates did not help to cure cost–push inflation even if they did not add demand–pull inflation to the situation.

What made the situation more difficult however was that industry was not responding very willingly to the signals to expand output: rather, existing stocks were being run down. Much of the new borrowing facilities were being taken up, not by industrialists, but by property dealers who were borrowing at very profitable rates (indeed at times at negative interest rates since the inflation rate was even greater than the interest rate), and in the process pushing up property values, particularly house prices.

The traditional relationships between an expansionist policy by government and the Bank of England, on the one hand, and the industrial sector on the other, were not working, or at least were not working as well as in the past. As a result the July measures took far longer to have any effect than had been expected.

This was indeed a time for testing of nerves among government ministers. It would have been very tempting to add in yet more measures but it was not likely that additional measures, however politically popular, would take effect quickly. Indeed the probability was that extra measures would have been irrelevant to the current situation, and very embarrassing in a year or two when their impact was felt.

What the government attempted over the next few months was to encourage a fair number of capital projects by local authorities, road improvements and the like, particularly in the regions of heavy unemployment, in the short term, without complicating the future by longer-term expenditure whose main effects would be felt for years.

In the process, however, one of the Conservative priorities was being frustrated. Public expenditure was rising again in spite of the long-term intention to cut this.

At this stage it might be useful to consider how the other priorities were faring. The one which looked most satisfactory was the balance of trade which was now almost embarrassingly healthy, particularly when the U.S. dollar found itself in difficulty and was allowed to float by the U.S. government.

The floating dollar brought no catastrophic results politically or economically to the U.S. economy – a fact which probably disarmed outside critics when sterling in turn was allowed to float the following year.

So far as regional policy was concerned, the main effects were felt through the short-term public sector spending on roads, etc., mentioned above. Since the major emphasis of this expenditure was on creating employment rather than efficient industry, the way was being opened for a rethinking of Conservative policy on the matter.

To what extent did the July measures work?

The turn round in the unemployment figures was agonisingly slow, and the appearance of the situation was not helped by the

seasonal rise in the unadjusted U.K. figures which were clearly
heading for a winter peak of over a million – a politically explosive figure.

What made the situation more piquant was that production,
which at first failed to respond to the stimulus, began in time to
move on to the 4–4.5 per cent growth forecast, but without a
corresponding rise in the numbers employed. Productivity was
rising, industry was becoming more efficient and shed labour
rather than recruiting more. In the long run, improved efficiency
is excellent: in the short run it was both unexpected and rather
embarrassing in view of what it was doing to the unemployment
figures.

The pattern for the rest of 1971 and the early part of 1972 is
shown in Table 12.

TABLE 12

	Industrial production	Retail prices	Annual % increase	Registered unemployed G.B. (s.a.) U.K. (unadjusted) Thousands		Balance of trade (s.a.) £ millions
1971						
Apr	126	152·2	9·4	704	513	16
May	126	153·2	9·8	731	794	28
June	126	154·3	10·3	741	762	− 48
July	125	155·2	10·2	788	830	+134
Aug	125	155·3	10·2	799	904	−231
Sep	126	155·5	9·9	793	929	59
Oct	125	156·4	9·4	807	930	38
Nov	125	157·3	9·3	838	970	− 2
Dec	125	158·1	9·0	858	967	37
1972						
Jan	125	159·0	8·2	802	1022	− 2
Feb[1]	112	159·8	8·1	n.a.	1003	− 34

The March 1972 Budget

The major factor in the March 1972 Budget was the unprecedented cuts in taxation, particularly in income tax. Total tax
cuts amounted, it was estimated, to over £1200 millions in the
1972–3 year. Since far and away the largest cuts came in income
tax the effects in increasing demand, and therefore output, could

[1] The February 1972 figures were distorted by the coal strike of the period.

be expected to be substantial. Once again it was apparent that the reduction of unemployment by a rapid expansion of the economy was intended.

The target output announced the previous July had been 4–4.5 per cent growth by mid-1972. Because of a crippling fuel strike early in the year it was now doubtful whether the target would be reached, or that, if it were, it would be at the lower level, i.e. about 4 per cent. Now the target was raised to 5 per cent annually between mid-1971 and mid-1973, i.e. by implication lost output would be made up and the rate of growth pushed up faster. This was a faster rate of growth over a longer period than probably had ever been achieved in modern times. The Chancellor, although still exercising caution over the longer term, was showing increasing confidence in giving hostages to fortune to publishing ambitious forecasts.

5 per cent growth was undoubtedly far above the prevailing growth of productive capacity. It has been argued that sustained growth may eventually raise productive potential, but the implications were inflationary in the short term. The background of this bold and potentially hazardous policy of massively increasing demand was that unemployment still rose inexorably. Government spokesmen were not prepared to give a clear-cut statement of exactly when the promised fall would take place or by how much; the historical precedents were all awry but there was little doubt that the turn round could not be much longer delayed if there was any validity at all in previous experience.

The interesting point about this very clear signal of priorities was that the new measures were as much symbolic in the short run as efficacious. Even though the tax cuts were almost all of the 'demand rich' variety, i.e. rapidly effected cuts in income tax, their main effects were not likely to be felt for months – or indeed possibly not until the following year. The turn round in unemployment, if and when it came, would depend on the working through of the earlier measures, principally those of nine months earlier.

Additionally there was yet another minor redistribution of national income by increased social security benefits matched by increased contributions.

The Budget was clearly designed with the immediate problems, particularly of unemployment and inflation, in mind;

there were, however, long-range plans for the reform of taxation and social security, commented on later.

The dominant feature of the next few months was that there were few real signs of developing industrial activity, at least so far as employment was concerned. What was happening was fairly clear. Productivity was still rising fairly fast so that the increased demand for labour did not materialise: in many instances too businessmen simply ran down stocks. But *why* this happened is not so clear, although the issue of low morale and pessimistic expectations of a future squeeze played their part. What was needed was a convincing demonstration that the government really would stick to its stated objective of rapid growth.

Such a demonstration did come in mid-year, with the rather unexpected sterling crisis. There had been very little comment on the good trade figures of the year 1971, after a period of marking time in 1970. All that could be said was that the external financial situation was not a constraint on expansion.

The background of the new crisis has been discussed in Chapter 9. The important point was that, given the choice of freezing the economy to save sterling, devaluing sterling or allowing it to float, the government chose the latter as being the alternative least likely to upset sustained growth in the economy. The pound floated down from $2.60 but industrial expansion was unchecked.

By the late summer the policy was beginning to show fruit.

TABLE 13

	Industrial production	Retail prices	Annual % increase	Registered unemployed G.B. (s.a.)	U.K. (unadjusted) Thousands	Balance of trade (s.a.) £ millions
1972						
Jan	125	159·0	8·2	862	1022	− 2
Feb	114	159·8	8·1	869	1003	− 34
Mar	127	160·3	7·6	879	1011	− 83
Apr	128	161·8	6·3	871	1002	− 50
May	131	162·6	6·1	834	901	− 43
June	130	163·7	6·1	798	833	+ 15
July	131	164·2	5·8	803	868	+ 30
Aug	130	165·5	6·6	807	929	−193
Sep	130	166·4	7·0	812	918	−136

Unemployment began to fall, fitfully at first, but to fall. The actual turn round had probably begun earlier in the year, but was only now becoming apparent, even in the seasonally adjusted figures.

The Move to a Statutory Incomes Policy

Once again it was possible to review the priorities. Unemployment had been contained. How did inflation stand? The answer was frankly not very encouraging, and the situation would have merited much earlier attention if unemployment had not been judged the greater political menace. What had happened primarily was that the government policy of encouraging a gradual fall in the size of wage settlements had been breached by the coal strike early in 1972 and an inflationary settlement, followed by other settlements almost as inflationary.

The effect of rising wage rates was likely to be worsened as actual earnings, including overtime, began to reflect the picking-up of industrial activity with less short time and more overtime. The steady fall in the foreign exchange rate for sterling, devaluation in fact if not in name, increased inflationary pressure.

Although the decision to float sterling rather than run down the reserves in the June crises undoubtedly saved a vast outflow of reserves as the trade figures plunged back into the red, the initial results of floating were certainly to worsen the next few months' figures as higher import bills arose from the depreciating pound long before there was any improvement from increased exports. But with output finally rising, and unemployment falling, the government was more concerned to sustain its success in these fields, even if this meant postponing for a time the problems implicit in the trade figures.

It is not the intention here to consider the extent of the government's *volte-face* as it moved from attempts at voluntary incomes limitations to a freeze and statutory policies, backed up by a Prices Commission and Pay Board.

But in one sense, though the results were transitorily humiliating to the government, there is probably more long-term significance in the less publicised aspect – the rearrangement of priorities. Most immediate was the evidence of the *pas de deux* between inflationary and unemployment counter-action. Inflation counter-measures had come to the front again with evidence

of a gentle credit squeeze, a slow down in the spectacular increase in the money supply, the calling in of special deposits by
the Bank of England, so as in effect to sterilise part of the commercial banks' holdings, the raising of interest rates : all of these
were indications that with unemployment contained for the moment, more attention could now go to inflation. But of particular
interest was the deliberate decision that the credit squeeze would
not be so severe as to check the 5 per cent growth target. The
immediate choice was no longer between growth and checking
inflation. Instead a new constraint had been added. The choice
was between growth at more than 5 per cent and checking inflation. Whether by political necessity or from choice, rapid
growth had emerged as the first priority, with the control of
inflation and the diminution of unemployment as second and
third priorities, in that order.

In a sense, given that the first priority was not negotiable, inflation and unemployment still caught the headlines and were
the major theme of the public debate. Table 14 (p. 183), showing how the situation was developing at the point of entry to
the E.E.C. on 1 January 1973, indicated that the inflationary
issue was still very much to the fore, even if the unemployment
situation was improving.

Where did the other objectives stand as Common Market
membership added a new dimension to the situation?

The stagnation of regional development, a by-product of unemployment was only too obvious. The results had been twofold :
first, a substantial revision of Conservative doctrine with financial aid being poured in more indiscriminatingly than ever before. In the process the Conservative ideal of cutting public expenditure had, in the short run at least, taken a severe knock.
There was little doubt that the Chancellor would be eager, as
soon as expedient, to reverse this. More promising, however,
was the attempt to manipulate the organisation of the European
Economic Community to produce a regional policy in that in-
stitution which would be of relevance to the U.K. problem.

Finally, a virtually uncovenanted good fortune, not merely in
its regional implications for employment, but in its national implications for the balance of payments, was the growing evidence
of oil and natural gas resources off Scotland, and also possibly
Wales.

Table 14 shows the situation at the end of 1972. At last there was evidence that industrial production was rising. The industrial production index figures were being revised upwards as more information became available and allowance was made for seasonal variation. At the same time G.D.P. as a whole was rising very rapidly though statistical proof would not be forthcoming on that fact for some months. Unemployment was clearly falling and the main weaknesses were in prices and the balance of payments.

TABLE 14

THE SITUATION AT THE END OF 1972

	Industrial production	Retail prices	Annual % increase	Registered unemployed G.B. (s.a.) U.K. (unadjusted) Thousands		Balance of trade (s.a.) £ millions
1972						
May	131	162·6	6·1	834	901	− 43
June	130	163·7	6·1	798	833	+ 15
July	131	164·2	5·8	803	868	+ 30
Aug	131	165·5	6·6	807	929	−193
Sep	133	166·4	7·0	812	918	−136
Oct	135	168·7	7·7	774	845	− 47
Nov	136	169·3	7·6	756	819	− 97
Dec	136	170·2	7·2	728	769	− 83

The next major strategic decision would presumably have to be the 1973 Budget and the appropriate action to be taken, particularly in respect of the level of V.A.T. which was to come into operation. Basically, however, the problems might be seen as threefold:

Would it be possible to continue the new rapid rate of growth?
Would it be possible to slow down inflation?
Would it be necessary to take action on the balance of payments?

So far as the first issue was concerned the government was already fairly heavily committed: arguably, too, rapid growth and therefore the hope of future wage increases were likely to some extent to make the wage restraints of the statutory income policy more acceptable to the trade unions.

The inflation issue depended on two factors: (i) internal costs – which it was hoped to check, if not control, through the new statutory bodies already mentioned, namely the Price Commission and the Pay Board; (ii) the course of world price fluctuations from which the United Kingdom could not be isolated. All the industrial countries were affected by inflation, and affected each other. The United Kingdom was perhaps more vulnerable than most because of her vast dependence on raw materials, the prices of which were moving up steadily, doubling overall during the year.

Finally a balance-of-trade deficit could be tolerated at least for the time being simply because a floating pound prevented a run on the reserves.

The March 1973 Budget

The indicators now stood as shown in Table 15.

TABLE 15

	Industrial production	Retail prices	Annual % increase	Registered unemployed G.B. (s.a.) U.K. (unadjusted) Thousands		Balance of trade (s.a.) £ millions
1972						
Nov	136	169·3	7·6	756	819	−97
Dec	136	170·2	7·2	728	769	−83
1973						
Jan	137	171·3	7·7	703	796	−77
Feb	138	172·4	7·9	660	746	−77

In the event the Budget was a broadly neutral one, with no substantial change in the level of taxation (V.A.T., being levied at 10 per cent, replaced other indirect taxes, mainly purchase tax); there were to be minor modifications on pensions, but the main intention was to allow the rapid 5 per cent growth target to be maintained for another year. The situation of price rises and the balance of payments depended on what success the incomes policy, now in its second phase, would have, and when the rise in raw material prices would be reversed. It was clear however that further fiscal changes would be introduced if they proved necessary later in the year.

During the next few months expansion appeared to be proceeding at a very rapid rate – probably as fast a rate as had ever been achieved by the British economy in a comparable time. But the figures tell the story of problems, as well as success : continuing, indeed rising, inflation and balance-of-trade deficits contrasting with rapid growth and falling unemployment.

TABLE 16

	Industrial production	Retail prices	Annual % increase	Registered unemployed G.B. (s.a.)	U.K. (unadjusted) Thousands	Balance of trade (s.a.) £ millions
1973						
Jan	137	171·3	7·7	703	796	− 77
Feb	138	173·4	7·9	660	746	− 77
Mar	140	173·4	8·2	630	712	−205
Apr	141	176·7	9·2	617	676	− 49
May	141	178·0	9·5	599	618	−209
June	141	179·9	9·3	590	571	−138
July	141	179·7	9·4	578	558	−159
Aug	141	180·2	8·9	565	559	−196
Sep	142	181·8	9·3	545	542	−178
Oct	142	185·4	9·9	515	528	−298

The major problems were in fact overseas. Mainly these related to the very rapid escalation in the costs of foodstuffs (accentuated slightly by the changeover to Common Market suppliers in some instances) and most other raw materials. In effect the government strategy of absorbing the high trade deficits was a gamble on the prospect of an equally rapid collapse of raw material prices – a reasonable gamble in view of the traditional pattern of such commodities but one where the timing was crucial.

The intention at the time was to hold the 5 per cent growth rate until about mid-1974 when it was anticipated that growth would slow gradually to about 3.5 per cent, i.e. about the same rate as the historical growth in productive capacity.

Once again, however, the plan went awry at the end of 1973. The outbreak of the Arab–Israeli conflict delayed the fall in raw material prices, and was followed by the Arab oil cuts which threatened the growth of virtually all the western economies. More serious in the long run was the effective co-operation of all the oil-producing nations to force up prices : a sixfold rise since

1970 and the prospect of more to come, with the more serious implications both on prices and balance-of-trade figures.

Because of the coincidence of more industrial disputes and wage claims in the mining industry, whose prospects had been transformed by the rise in oil prices, the British situation looked about as grim as any of the industrial countries. In fact in the longer term the United Kingdom was probably better placed than most, having a large and viable coalmining industry and the prospect of virtual self-sufficiency in domestic oil supplies in a few years. The immediate implications, however, were that once again rapid growth would have to be postponed, and a large deficit in overseas trade coped with. A new strategy, and new selection of priorities, was going to be required – probably for some five years – until adequate fuel supplies from domestic sources could free the economy from the balance-of-trade constraint.

The Fall of the Conservative Government, February–March 1974

The government's term of office came to an end when the Conservatives lost the General Election in February 1974.

Table 17 shows how the economic indicators were standing at that time. Industrial production had slowed down – and was about to fall due to the economic situation. Both inflation and the balance-of-trade figures were visibly worsening and only the unemployment figures were moving in the right direction. The implication of the rapid escalation in import prices, particularly oil prices, was that the next year or two would see less prospect of growth and a recurrence of the chronic balance-of-trade problems which had been such a feature of most of the post-war period.

The decision to call the election was triggered by renewed industrial action by the miners, first a 'go-slow' and then an all-out strike, whose settlement would almost inevitably wreck the statutory incomes policy introduced the previous year. The strength of the miners' situation had been increased enormously, if possibly temporarily, by the scarcity and high price of oil.

The decision to call the election in these circumstances, long before Parliament had run its constitutional course, was controversial – the more so when the results were known. The Opposition fought their campaign on a voluntary incomes policy, backed by severer price controls. Their so-called 'Social Contract' between trade unions and government depended on the proposition that the trade unions would not add to inflation by excessive and competitive wage claims.

Both major political parties had tried voluntary incomes policies – and failed : both had tried statutory incomes policies, one had withdrawn under trade union hostility, the other had failed to convince the electorate that this was the best way. But the implication was that if the new attempt at voluntary constraints did not work, the choice would lie between even faster inflation and even higher unemployment than the nation had experienced before in the post-war years.

TABLE 17

	Industrial production	Retail prices	Annual % increase	Registered unemployed G.B. (s.a.) U.K. (unadjusted) Thousands		Balance of trade (s.a.) £ millions
1973						
Aug	141	180·2	8·9	565	559	−193
Sep	142	181·8	9·3	545	542	−176
Oct	142	185·4	9·9	515	528	−357
Nov	139	186·8	10·3	490	518	−270
Dec	135	188·2	10·6	467	509	−328

PART III

CONTROLLING THE ECONOMY

This section discusses the relatively sophisticated machinery which is available to a British government to control the economy: that is, to achieve the objectives outlined in the previous section. It can be said at once that the results achieved are often far from those attempted.

The failure in performance is perhaps most marked over the whole question of demand management, the attempt to control the pace of economic growth so that a steady growth of output can be achieved which neither leaves a substantial amount of slack in the economy, nor at the same time produces a headlong rush into an inflationary situation in an overstimulated economy. Why has demand management been so often out of step with the real requirements of the economy? Why, if productive capacity is growing by about 3 to 3.5 per cent per annum cannot sustained and substainable growth at that rate be achieved? The actual performance in demand management has in fact been so poor in the post-war years that it has been argued that attempts to control it, instead of 'letting nature take its course', have been positively harmful.

It is probable that, whatever else has gone wrong, the economic theory, particularly the Keynesian model built up, has been sound enough to indicate appropriate action. The trouble briefly has not been in the theory but in the application of that theory, particularly because of the limitations on accurate information about what is actually going on in the economy. A very pertinent observation made about the British economy is always to know where it is now. Time and time again it becomes apparent that a significant turning point, a change from a rise to a fall in unemployment, or exports, or of any number of other economic indicators, comes and goes without anyone being aware, until months later, when the turning point is.

This might seem an extraordinary state of affairs. Certainly it is not the sort of situation envisaged in a theoretical model of the economy where inputs and outputs can be measured and timed with precision.

In a real-life messy situation when thousands, perhaps millions, of individuals are making decisions which affect the national economy the last thing that is on their minds is the problem of signalling their intentions to the authorities who are trying to measure what is happening. Most of the practical difficulties have already been spelt out, possibly *ad nauseam*. But if they are overlooked then the economic planners or prognosticators are in trouble. These difficulties are, therefore, worth repetition.

First, information is not immediately available to the central government because no one is really interested or concerned to make it available. The significant information accumulates weeks or even months after the events it measures : even as it becomes available, the early indications may have to be substantially revised. No one can say for sure within a few hundred million what is the G.D.P. for the United Kingdom for any quarter until many weeks after the end of the period, and still the preliminary estimates will be a mixture of hard information, estimates and downright guesswork. Even information which is collected for its own sake, not as a by-product, requires the goodwill of the people who are asked to supply it, regardless of any legal sanctions which may apply.

The situation in dealing with turning points in the economy is made more complicated by the problem of seasonally adjusted information. It is probable that a large number of people who are reading off the indicators still do not realise the extent to which seasonal adjustments both aid and confuse an appreciation of the situation. Seasonal adjustments are made to figures to produce an overall trend which will not be obscured by the regular seasonal variations. The fact that more people get jobs in April of any year does not indicate anything about the overall picture, any more than the fact that seasonal workers may lose jobs in October or November inevitably means that unemployment overall is rising. To that extent seasonally adjusted figures of, say, unemployment are more meaningful than month by month comparisons of raw figures. But it is only too easy to take the phrase 'seasonally adjusted' for granted. How in fact have the figures been seasonally adjusted? By being averaged out over the year, by a more sophisticated mathematical treatment, by hunch, or what? The more sophisticated and mathematically sound the methods used, the more observations have to be included in the calculations. But are, for example, August unemployment figures of two or three years back all that relevant to what is happening this year? The very sophistication of techniques tends to obscure the really significant fact that seasonal adjustment depends on what has happened in the past: the further back go the figures which are used in seasonal adjustments, the longer it will be before seasonally adjusted figures throw up significant information about a turning point. And a turning point in the economy really means that the figures for the past months have suddenly become irrelevant if not downright misleading. All calculations are only as good as the raw material: and the raw material for economic decisions is only too often inaccurate or out of date at the critical moment when significant decisions to expand or contract demand ought to be made.

In a democratic society the government has surprisingly little 'hard' up-to-date information on which to base policy. Turning points in the economic situation are almost inevitably seen in hindsight – and even then the uncertainty existing at the time gets blurred in recall. The only consolation is that in a totalitarian society the information is probably worse, because although the information can be demanded from the economic sectors, its quality is probably a good deal more suspect, for people are tempted to report what it is expedient to report.

CHAPTER 11

THE MEANS OF CONTROL

THERE are conventionally two means whereby an economy's level of demand can be controlled: firstly, by monetary policy, which may be defined as an attempt to control the amount of purchasing power which is made available to the community; secondly, by fiscal means, i.e. using the fact of taxation and public expenditure. At its most extreme, fiscal policy can be allied to physical controls, licensing, rationing and the like.

Monetary Policy

A good deal can be written about the somewhat arcane method whereby a government through a central bank (i.e. the Bank of England) can arrange to increase or diminish the supply of money circulating in our economy. By permitting the money supply to increase, the Bank of England, operating through the commercial banks and indirectly through other financial institutions, can ensure that industry, commerce or the private individual can, if necessary, borrow relatively easily and so increase the demand for goods and services. Alternatively, by imposing severe controls on the money supply, the Bank can make money both scarcer and dearer to cut down economic activity if expansion or inflation threatens to get out of hand.

It is not proposed in a book of this nature to discuss the technicalities in detail. It may suffice however to make the obvious point that money supply extends far beyond the quantity of bank-notes and coins. Most transactions outside personal day-to-day purchases do not involve the physical paying over of bank-notes by one individual to another. They are carried out by the use of cheques or similiar financial instruments. The actual money supply at any one time is probably four or five times as great as the actual physical supply of money. In this sense bank-notes and coins are convenient but not the essential item in the various components of the money supply.

It is not all that easy to define precisely what is the money supply. The most conventional definition is M₃, that is to say bank-notes and coins outside the banks plus all resident deposits in the U.K. banking sector (i.e. those deposits which can be used as the basis for bank credits). In passing it might be said that the other more strict definition of the money supply M₁ is of more limited use, and that an intermediate M₂ definition has passed out of use.

Two points ought to be made about M₃. Because of the way in which foreign lending transactions are absorbed into the economy, an inflow of overseas funds tends to increase the supply – unless, that is, the Bank of England takes steps to counter this by contracting M₃ in a compensating degree elsewhere. Equally the withdrawal of foreign funds tends to contract the money supply – again unless the Bank of England chooses to counter this effect. The Bank of England therefore is not the sole arbiter of the money supply although it may choose to correct the effects of activities such as the inflow or outflow of foreign funds, if it feels the movement is against internal economic requirements.

The second point is that the money supply, in so far as it can be used to counter, or add to, inflation, does so on the assumption that the inflation is of the demand–pull variety. This, as has been seen, is the justification for the argument that it is possible to reflate without significantly adding to inflation, i.e. on the assumption that the typical inflation of the 1970s is cost–push, extending the money supply does not fuel the inflationary process unless and until money supply expands so fast as to create demand–pull inflation in addition.

Monetary policy as an instrument of control has both advantages and disadvantages. The main advantage is that it is possible to exercise virtually day-to-day control – or more strictly week-by-week, by taking steps to vary the amount of money or money equivalent in the market. The main disadvantage is that it is essentially indiscriminate and is liable to have a blunderbuss effect since there is no guarantee that extra purchasing power will be used in the desired manner, e.g. for investment rather than for property speculation, or conversely that if the money supply is being cut, the appropriate economic activity will be hit. A certain amount of control may be attempted, but it is frankly extremely difficult to ensure that they work, short of a very rigid form of licensing.

G

Fiscal Policy

The second major instrument of demand management is the use of fiscal policy – otherwise known as budgetary policy. The point has already been made that the Budget, which was until about a generation ago simply a means of collecting sufficient revenue by way of taxation to meet the everyday needs of government, has now several more roles. Among these is the role of redistributing national income by 'progressive' taxation, i.e. the practice of making the better-off sections of the community bear more than a proportional share of taxation, and the less well-off a lesser share. And connected indirectly with this but of more consequence in the present discussion is the role of regulating demand.

Briefly, and at the risk of considerable oversimplification, the Budget lays down for the following year the quantities of taxation and public expenditure, i.e. T and G in our original model. The earlier concept of a balanced Budget in practice meant that T and G would be equal, that is to say a financially neutral Budget. But in the present role of the Budget it is accepted that it is permissible that current taxation and current expenditure need not balance. A deficit Budget, i.e. less being collected than is being spent (the deficit being made up by borrowing), means that G exceeds T and has a multiplier effect, either raising the level of national income in real terms or, if the Budget fails to get the desired result, creating more inflation. Similarly a surplus Budget where taxation T exceeds current spending is deflationary in effect because the target T is a leakage, which is presumably greater than that which would have been achieved by S (savings) or M (imports).

The fiscal policy can in theory increase or decrease the pressure of demand.

In the original model neither T (taxation) nor G (government or public expenditure) was defined too closely because it is in practice difficult to determine precisely the leakage or multiplier effect of individual taxes or payments. The situation is made rather more opaque by the convention that, normally, current expenditure should be covered by taxation and extraordinary expenditure by borrowing – the device for this borrowing being the National Debt which was created as a device for financing the extraordinary expenses of the eighteenth-century Anglo-French wars. The obsolescent but useful terms were above- and below-the-line expenditure. Deficit budgeting implies that even routine above-the-line expenditure may in part be financed by borrowing, while surplus budgeting means part or all of the annual below-the-line expenditure being met from current taxation.

Common sense should tell the reader when deficit budgeting with its risk of inflation might seem a sensible move: putting it into the model form, why the government should want taxation T to be as low as possible. Conversely of course when surplus budgeting is the order, T contains an element of forced savings.

But as well as affecting the overall *pressure* of demand, fiscal policy can be used to affect the *pattern* of demand. Taxation is not just an overall concept. It can be applied discriminately to encourage or discourage certain activities, reward certain sectors of the community and so on. Some of the implications are traced out in the next sections, so far as directing both taxation and public expenditure are concerned.

As everyone knows, the Budget is an annual event with an element of cup-final tension as commentators analyse the somewhat unpromising prose of the Chancellor of the Exchequer. But there is in the whole process a certain amount of meaningless ceremony and, more important, some self-imposed restraints. The Budget Statement leads to a Finance Bill, and is an annual event for constitutional rather than financial reasons: in the past the necessity for an annual grant of taxation power represented an essential element of Parliamentary power.

The constitutional battle has been won however and the annual nature of the event is as much historical as financial. It is, of course, perfectly possible to have an autumn Budget as well as the spring one. But such an event is normally seen as a crisis and a measure of failure of economic policy; or a new government may choose to have a new Budget so as to be able to change course without waiting a full year.

Stability and certainty in finance are important; but one of the disadvantages of fiscal policy is that normally it is changed only annually, if at all. There might be a case for arguing that overall fiscal policy could be laid down once a year (or possibly at an even longer interval) but that mini-budgets, say every two or

three months, to introduce an element of flexibility could be
accepted as a normal event, rather than a sign of an emergency. Certainly a case can be made out both for fiscal policy
being set for several years in advance rather than one year,
and at the opposite extreme for frequent changes every few
months.

The argument for the former is that uncertainty is the enemy
of sustained growth, and that therefore if a government were
ready and able to give an undertaking that whatever happened
no change would be made in some aspects of fiscal policy for two
or three years, it might overcome the mistrust of government
financial policies which possesses so much of British industry,
after years of chopping and changing.

The argument for the frequent change has already been
stated : basically it is that in a dynamic society, a turning point in
the economy from say rising to falling employment cannot be
allowed to go unremarked for up to a year at a time. In some
ways more flexibility is being introduced into the system in two
ways. The government is now, on occasion, prepared to alter
fiscal policy by fresh legislation in midstream so to speak without
the paraphernalia of the Budget ritual, without even calling the
changes a new Budget. Secondly, since the 1960s governments
have used 'regulator' powers, that is they have provided in the
Finance Bill, which puts the year's Budget proposals into effect,
that some taxes may be altered by up to 10 per cent without fresh
legislation having to be introduced. This regulator obviously
erodes the principle of Parliamentary control of finance, but it
does add to flexibility in the economy which is becoming increasingly dynamic not to say downright volatile.

It may well be that the Budget mechanism will evolve in both
directions, with, for example, corporation tax or its equivalents,
tax rebates on investments and the like – measures which affect
the long-term budget decisions – either being set for several years
in advance, or with changes being signalled a year or two ahead
so that planned investment will really be planned; but on the
other hand other forms of taxation which have a more immediate
effect on the level of the economy, i.e. 'demand rich' taxes, might
be subject to more frequent changes. The administrative complexities of such frequent changes would be enormous. But a
fiscal system, born out of constitutional necessities a few

centuries ago and refined to meet the leisurely economic pace of the nineteenth century, might justifiably be regarded as increasingly inappropriate for a vastly more complex and dynamic society.

This is a somewhat speculative look at the problem. At the moment, however, the point about fiscal policy is that its advantages and disadvantages are the mirror image of monetary policy. It can be made very selective both in the incidence and the amount of taxation falling on any section of the community or any economic activity which is to be encouraged or discouraged. But conversely it is slow in working through – in the case of the 'demand poor' taxes, which essentially affect company investment decisions, the effects may take several years to work out. Even 'demand rich' tax changes on consumption take perhaps months to work out. It is a convenient fiction that each year's Budget starts with a clean slate : in fact the effects of previous Budgets are in the background affecting the whole picture. Some of these effects may not have begun to be felt until one or more subsequent Budgets and their Finance Bills have gone on to the Statute Book.

After the brief if somewhat discursive look at the overall imlications of fiscal policy it will be useful to look separately at the two sides to fiscal policy, namely taxation and expenditure.

Taxation

In general this discussion will be confined to what the general public thinks of as taxation, e.g. income tax, tax on wines, beers, spirits, tobacco, etc. There are other methods of raising revenue for more specific purposes, namely local rates and national insurance contributions. These however can be treated in an elementary discussion of this kind as merely a variety of taxation, levied on a slightly different basis than the central government taxation.

The proportion of national income appropriated by the government in the form of taxation is probably about 30 per cent of the total. Some of this however is in the form of transfer payments of national income from the better-off to the poorer sections of the community. The general trend is for the proportion to rise, and although Conservative governments in general tend to try to cut taxation, while Labour governments feel more disposed to public sector spending and redistribution of wealth, the overall tendency is upwards.

A useful broad division of taxation, with both economic and political implications, is the division into direct and indirect taxation. Direct taxation (for example, income tax, corporation tax on company profits, capital gains tax), is, as the phrase suggests, levied directly on earnings or incomes. It tends to be progressive, i.e. it can be pitched so that the burden is heavier on the better-off rather than the poor, on dividends, profits, interest receipts than on wages and salaries, and so forth. There is an element of social redistribution of wealth implied in these taxes.

The main disadvantage is that they may appear to act as a disincentive to earn more income. The abolition of surtax, which was paid over and above income tax until the early 1970s, has perhaps lessened this argument, but the fact remains that at a high enough level income tax may be at 90 per cent or more.

The alternative method is indirect taxation; in the past an obvious example was purchase tax. In the 1970s the most obvious example is V.A.T. (value added tax) first introduced in 1973. Indirect taxes of this sort are taxes on *consumption* rather than income. In a sense consumers have the choice of paying or not paying except where these fall on necessities. The advantage of indirect taxation is that being a tax on consumption it is not so likely to act as a disincentive. Even if a section of the population feel that taxation is too high they may still choose to earn and save against the hope of lower taxes in the future. Incidentally therefore indirect taxes may affect the propensity to save.

The major disadvantage is social, in that the same amount of tax, at least on the same goods, is paid by rich and poor alike. In order to maintain administrative simplicity V.A.T. rates are kept as uniform as possible, and therefore it is not easy to put a more than proportional rate on luxuries and a less than proportional rate on necessities. The choice is between having products pay or be exempted or zero rated, although the effect of the latter is not so sweeping in its effects. Absolute necessities, e.g. most types of food, can be exempted, but the overall effect is rather regressive than progressive.

Again, at the risk of oversimplification, it can be said that Conservative governments have a preference for indirect, and Labour governments for direct taxation. But nowadays in spite of the political declamations there is a broad measure of common ground and the political preferences for direct or indirect taxation should not be pushed too far.

Rates are the form of taxation levied by local authorities under fairly strict control by the central government. They are essentially property taxes paid by the house owner or rentee, or by industrial concerns. In that sense since they are not universal it is a little difficult to define them as being progressive or regressive. Much depends not only on the level of the rate charge, but on the rateable value put on the property on which the rates are levied, and on the proportion of municipally owned housing on which less than economic rents are paid, within the district. A high proportion of council housing which may be let out at less than an economic rent, with the difference being largely made up out of rates on privately owned property, is a form of redistribution of national income, progressive in theory if not in practice. The difficulty is that not all the less well-off live in council houses to benefit from this redistribution, and not all council house dwellers are to be counted among the less well-off. Rates, their incidence and size, are political hot potatoes, and the central government whatever its political complexion is always liable to find itself at odds with rate-levying councils of a different political complexion. Indeed it is quite possible to find central government and local governments working at cross purposes particularly so far as the distribution of national income is concerned. Since, however, the central government through the Budget provides about half the local authorities' funds, the former is likely to prevail in the long run.

Finally national insurance contributions, being partly a lump sum weekly and partly a supplement, are in part at least regressive rather than progressive as a form of taxation. Since however a large proportion is paid by employers rather than employees, there is another progressive element superimposed here, although not on the contributions of the self-employed or the non-employed who are not of retiring age. Two points arise on national insurance as a form of taxation. The total revenue is not sufficient to cover the entire cost of social security, some 20 to 25 per cent coming from a central government grant. Secondly, as has been noted earlier, contributory pensions are something of a misnomer in the sense that contributions paid in the past cannot affect directly the cost of pensions paid in the present, both because the value of money has changed but more importantly because a transfer income payment in the current year can only be achieved at the expense of some other demand this year.

It might seem to be wandering from the point in a discussion about taxation to dwell on the issue of social security. But an interesting development in recent years which has most profound implications has been the tendency for taxation and social security to become mirror images one of the other.

The most important example of the overlap is probably the increasing interest in the concept, mentioned earlier, of negative income tax. It might seem to be nonsense to talk of a tax which puts more purchasing power into the hands of those whom it affects, rather than less. The basic argument for a negative income tax is that it represents a minimum allowance to which everyone in society would be entitled, so that it would be a grant if a person's income was below the limit and a tax allowance if the income were above it. There are plenty of snags about the concept, political and social, but the big advantage of the system is that it might enable the worst paid sections of society to obtain an acceptable standard of living without having every other wage and salary earner demanding equivalent and inflationary increases to maintain differentials. For it is one of the most potent factors of industrial behaviour that most people are as much concerned with how much more they get than someone less skilled or qualified, than with their absolute income.

Political Aspects of Taxation. There is a good deal of common ground between the two major political parties about social aims in the community. But though the differences might seem marginal compared with those prevalent in some other parts of the world, they are the very stuff of political debate. They can be summarised thus :

(a) How far does the community wish progressive taxation to be carried?

(b) Allied with this, should the emphasis be placed on direct or indirect taxation? And if on direct taxation to what extent should it be carried by the company sector and how much by individuals?

(c) Again linked with the first two, is there a general feeling of overtaxation, particularly overtaxation to the point where individuals genuinely feel that the tax structure puts an obstacle on individual effort?

The Phenomenon of Fiscal Drag. The overall effect of taxation in western society is that it is in general progressive, and therefore any rise in income is likely to produce a more than proportionate rise in the revenue arising from taxation. In a situation of virtually endemic inflation this means that as *money* incomes rise throughout the year through inflation, the incidence of tax rises too. This phenomenon of fiscal drag is a built-in check which tends to limit the effect of inflation by mopping up more of the increased purchasing power.

A politically useful effect from a government's point of view is that without actually raising tax levels in money terms, merely by leaving these unchecked it raises the level in real terms. Putting this another way a minor consolation of inflation is that successive budgets can cut taxation in money terms while retaining it at the original level in real terms. This as has has been noted had become something of a regular feature in the early 1970s.

Public Expenditure

A distinction has already been drawn between factor and transfer incomes; so far as the latter are concerned, the obverse of factor incomes is that proportion of public expenditure which is simply a device for transferring national income as between one sector of the public and another.

The major type of public expenditure – the *G* of our model – is however that type of expenditure which represents a claim on national resources, and this, as has been remarked, consumes about 30 per cent of national product.

But in so far as public expenditure on this scale has a very profound effect on the whole economy it is worth considering the extent to which such expenditure can be compared with expenditure by the individual or the individual commercial or industrial enterprise. The major factor is that so far as public expenditure is concerned the true cost may be very hard to establish because of the repercussions throughout the economy. Putting it at its simplest, what is the true cost to the economy of say £10 millions in building naval vessels?

There are a variety of situations which can be envisaged.

H

First, where there is very heavy unemployment and spare shipbuilding capacity. Then at the extreme in real terms the cost might be virtually nil if the result was that labour and production facilities which would otherwise be idle were used. Here, since national resources are not being diverted from any other use, the opportunity cost, i.e. the value of the alternative products which would otherwise have been produced, is nil, regardless of the money cost of £10 million.

In a situation where there was some underutilisation of resources then there would be a real cost, which would not however be as great as the money cost, since only part of the opportunity cost would be at the expense of alternative use of resources. To put this in more concrete terms, if such expenditure resulted in an increase in employment, then we would not have to count the *total* of the wages paid out to the newly employed : we would be entitled to deduct the cost of unemployment benefits which would otherwise have been paid, and also make an allowance for the extra tax revenue which would be paid by the former recipients.

Finally only in a situation of absolutely full utilisation of resources would the opportunity cost approach the money cost. Here £10 million expenditure on ships would mean £10 million less production and expenditure elsewhere, and incidentally the diversion of resources might have a very complex consequence, affecting the distribution of national income to the various factors of production and causing changes in the pattern of taxation which might affect the amount of tax revenue to be set against the money cost.

Public Expenditure – Semi-transfer Payments

Earlier a distinction was made between factor and transfer payments, namely payments to factors of production or their owners and controllers (wages and salaries, rents, dividends and the like) on the one hand, and pensions and similar payments on the other, whose main intent was to transfer purchasing power from one section of the community to another for social reasons.

It has been convenient here, as so often before, to assume that it is possible to distinguish clearly between factor and transfer payments, and that therefore when discussing public expenditure (G in our model) we could confine the term to payments which gave rise to factor incomes. Again, as so often in real life, the distinction can become blurred and the real-life situation a good deal more difficult to represent than a theoretical model.

The main difficulty arises with subsidies, housing or food, for example. Arguably a householder living in a council house subsidised by local or central government funds is enjoying a transfer of income from the people who are paying the actual and economic rent, in the form of either taxation or rates. Again subsidised food means that the consumer is paying less than the real cost. But some confusion might arise in defining a food subsidy as a transfer income, because presumably everyone is paying less for food, not merely a particular group. Everyone eats, but not everyone lives in a subsidised council house.

One can of course with logic maintain that a food subsidy is still a transfer payment although *everyone* feels the benefit in lower prices, some people gain more than others, i.e. cheap food benefits the less well-off more than the well-to-do, who are paying more of the subsidy through taxation. Although the logic still holds, the thread is slightly harder to follow.

What happens if a government decides to make more routine payments to the nationalised industries or other units in the private or public sector, for reasons other than to assist investment? For example, if in an attempt to hold down prices the central authorities urge the nationalised industries or the public utilities to sell their services, e.g. rail transport or electrical power, below cost price, generally by holding prices steady during an inflationary period, then this is a form of subsidy designed to offer services to industry or the general public at below the real cost. The subsidy however still comes from some section or another of the public, and effectively therefore a transfer payment is being made. It would again be very convenient if governments categorised exactly the purpose of public expenditure of this sort, e.g. $£X$ millions of a public sector payment to be for purposes of investment, $£Y$ to keep the costs of the services as charged to customers down, and then it would be possible to make the distinction and perhaps quantify the effects. Of course governments in making grants and public sector authorities in accepting them make no very accurate distinction. But the fact that elements of both factor and transfer payments are involved is yet one more reason why it is virtually impossible to put exact measurements on the quantities involved in a real life mode. G is, empirically, about two-thirds of all public expenditure – that is about the only degree of accuracy which can be achieved at present in a real-life situation.

Physical Controls

The logical end of fiscal policy, if pushed far enough, is the use of physical controls to restrain demand, that is to say the use of licensing quotas or rationing. Clearly in this context physical controls are effective only as a brake on excess demand; as a means of stimulating demand they are virtually useless.

In western Europe, physical controls as a part of demand management are virtually unknown in peacetime. In part there appears to be a political revulsion against them as a relic of war and post-war hardship. An administrative objection to them is the problem of effectiveness or expense. Virtually any type of control can be evaded, if sufficient ingenuity is misapplied, and the authorities have therefore to decide how rigid the controls must be, how elaborate the machinery to prevent evasion and, most delicate of all, what legal sanctions to use against evaders. The exercise of physical controls varies between the Scylla of ineffectiveness and the danger of bringing the law into disrepute, and the Charybdis of draconian punishments against offenders where the severity of the punishment far exceeds the gravity of what many people might not even regard as a crime.

The nearest parallels to such permanent controls in the past few years have been the various foreign-exchange controls and the occasional emergency statutory powers to control wages, etc. The controls in both cases were probably never absolutely watertight, the authorities being content to make evasion very difficult except for the most determined.

It is difficult to believe that extensive and permanent physical controls to supplement fiscal policy could become a regular weapon in the Chancellor's armoury, without something like wartime conditions to justify the penal sanctions implied. Such controls in war and its aftermath produced the 'spiv' and the illegal 'fixer' who know where and how to evade controls. The 'fixer' in this sense is a despised but possibly essential adjunct of the controlled economies of eastern Europe. Human nature being as it is, controls work effectively only if there is unofficially available a person or a system which can evade the system in an emergency.

Monetary and Fiscal Policy

The reader may feel that a good deal of emphasis has been laid on the contrasts between the two major instruments of control. Certainly, as has been remarked, there are political preferences in the use of these, but governments of both political parties have used both methods in conjunction. The emphasis has of course changed. In the immediate post-war period of reconstruction, monetary policy was relatively neglected. A cheap money policy to reduce the cost of reconstruction, particularly to the public sector, formed a neutral background with an elaborate pattern of fiscal and physical controls as the main instruments. As a reaction the Conservative governments of the 1950s and early 1960s swung violently in the opposite direction : it would probably be fair to say that the pattern since then has been of successive governments dramatically reversing their predecessors' priorities and gradually, as the disadvantages of their chosen instruments began to appear, quietly reintroducing the alternative policy to supplement the earlier.

One relatively unremarked casualty of the 1960s was the concept of fine tuning, one example of which might be the attempt to use one policy to set the general level of demand, and then to use the other to make fine adjustments. In the present volatile state of the British economy, the idea of any very fine adjustment is rather a myth. Demand management, using the complementary tools of monetary and fiscal policies, still remains a very hit or miss affair.

CHAPTER 12

FORECASTING AND PLANNING
THE FUTURE

As has been seen, virtually any economic activity by a central government, short of a physical shut-down of an industry, takes a long time to mature. Sometimes many months pass, conceivably several years. During the time when the original policy is working through the economy subsequent policy decisions overlap, distort or conceal the effects, for the very mundane reason that all sorts of actions have to be taken before anyone really knows what the effects of the earlier decisions are going to be.

The dangers of analogy in economics have been stressed, but an appropriate concept might be of the British economy as a super-tanker of hundreds of thousands of tons having to weave its way through unknown waters – the future. The tanker at any speed takes several miles to overcome its own momentum if a turn has to be made when an obstacle is seen looming up ahead; and it may be a long time before the most frantic spinning of the wheel will have any obvious effect. If the obstacle can be seen only at very close range and there is no hope of avoiding it at speed, the only alternative may be to reverse engines and try to stop the vessel dead before it comes to disaster; even so, stopping the vessel at immense strain to the whole structure might take too long. In the circumstance the master mariner may be compelled to move very slowly indeed, far more slowly than the designed cruising speed of the vessel, rather than risk disaster. Even when the way ahead seems clear again it may take a very long time to pick up speed.

In this analogy, with the ship's engines representing productive capacity, the speed of the ship is the rate of growth of national product. The designed speed represents the 3–3.5 per cent growth in productive capacity; only too often actual growth is below this, because obstacles in the future cannot be foreseen in time.

Obviously in such a situation, whether in terms of unknown

waters lying ahead of the ship, or unknown economic events lying ahead of the economy, the more the unknown element can be
reduced the safer rapid progress can become. In economic terms
forecasting represents the attempt to predict and quantify what
is going to happen : not only to predict what is going to happen if
government policy remains unchanged, but more profitably what
are the probable consequences of various hypothetical moves –
alternative scenarios to use a somewhat exotic phrase.

It is useful in forecasting to distinguish between three periods
of time.

Conventionally *short-term forecasting* can be defined as an
attempt to project the probable course of events over say
eighteen months to two years. This represents a period when
there is not likely to be any unforeseen change in the productive
capacity of the economy (the productive capacity being already
in existence or in an advanced stage of creation); moreover the
effects of tax policies in the past will largely have worked themselves through the economy.

Medium-term forecasting would represent a period of say up
to five to seven years ahead, where there is time for important
investment decisions, not yet taken, to be taken and to have their
effects on the productive potential before the period is over.
For example the present productive capacity fixed in the short
term at 3–3.5 per cent might have fallen to a new equilibrium of
say 2 per cent or risen to say 6 per cent. But even where productive potential could have changed the technology at the end of
the five-to-seven-year period it might reasonably be regarded as
predictable and recognisable today, i.e. there would be no
miraculous technological breakthrough which would transform
the economy beyond recognition

Long-term forecasting – perhaps for a generation ahead – is
frankly speculation. Political economic and above all technological change is accelerating and all one can reasonably forecast for say the year A.D. 2000 is that it will be quite different
from present guesses on the subject.

In practical, i.e. in realisable political and economic terms,
forecasting is a vital tool of demand management in the short
term, very important for the overall direction of the economy in
the medium term and desirable but unreliable for more than
about a decade ahead.

Short-term Forecasting

There are essentially two methods which can be used for short-term forecasting : (a) the use of econometric and mathematical techniques, (b) opinion gathering, i.e. a sort of grass-roots approach.

Forecasting using mathematical techniques is probably the most widely acceptable activity under this general heading. In principle it is little different from the idea of manipulating raw figures to achieve seasonally adjusted series : indeed a simple seasonally adjusted series becomes a forecast merely by extending the trend, by drawing it in by hand if necessary on a graph. In recent years, however, the techniques have become immensely more complex for two interconnected reasons.

First, the widespread introduction of computers has made possible immensely more complex calculations. Thus, for example, before the availability of computers it was generally necessary to handle aggregated material, i.e. to work in grand totals such as the output of entire industries, trusting that internal errors or inaccuracies in the material would tend to cancel out. Now it is possible to disaggregate, i.e. to break up overall information on an industry into virtually individual factory units, perform relatively simple but tedious and inordinate numbers of calculations by computer and aggregate the innumerable parts to give a more accurate whole.

Secondly, the availability of computers to deal with the minutiae of statistics has made possible the output of economic statistical material, the raw material for the complex calculations.

The same two conditions have produced a vast expansion in the application of mathematical and statistical techniques to economics in general, and the distinction between econometrics and forecasting of this sort is blurred. Economic forecasters in this area are often econometricians or statisticians by training.

Notwithstanding what has been said above, a short-term forecasting model is not necessarily entirely mathematical in nature. There is almost inevitably an element of subjective judgement about the values to be allocated to information fed into the most mathematical model; or again in evaluating the answers thrown up by the model. In constructing the econometric model which is going to process the raw statistics the forecaster is in a chicken and egg situation. The relationships which make up the model are based on what are regarded as the most significant historical relationships and the relationships within the model may be amended in the light of fresh statistical information which the model is processing. It would be unrealistic to assume that even the most accomplished econometricians and statisticians could easily produce a mathematical model of the British economy in terms perhaps of hundreds of interconnected equations, or that, having done so, they could assume that the same relationships held good for year after year. In other words human judgement comes into the contents of the forecasting model, and how often and how much the model has got to be amended if and when the forecasts turn out to differ from the actual outcome. Theoretical models have constantly to be adjusted to correspond more closely with reality.

The further the results are to be projected into the future the more important becomes the judgement factor at the expense of the mathematical technique.

Unfortunately however there is a complication. The implication that one can rely more securely on mathematical techniques in short-term forecasting has to be balanced against a disadvantage which becomes more acute the shorter the forecasting period involved. This disadvantage arises from the doubtful accuracy of the most up-to-date information, and conversely the doubtful freshness of really accurate information. It might seem ridiculous to argue that one is never quite sure what is happening to an economy, *when* it happens. Information only becoming available today refers to conditions weeks or months in the past. A 6-months' forecast using very accurate, i.e. out-of-date, information is in a sense a 12-months' forecast since it is starting with 6-months-old information; the true 6-months' forecast would merely give an opinion about what is happening today.

The depressing point about mathematically based forecasting, even in the short term, is that as often as not it is awry in its results. This is frankly a very worrying situation, not merely in view of the expense and the calibre of the persons involved but, far more important, for the political consequences. Any government in the run-up to a general election desperately needs to get its economic strategy right on election day, and as has been said earlier can in a limited sense so dispose its strategy as to get the

H*

economic results it wants at about the right time. An inaccurate short-term forecast and the wrong short-term measures could cost a government a general election. Arguably this happened to the Conservative government in 1964 and the Labour government in 1970.

Why do forecasts go wrong so spectacularly in spite of the sophisticated techniques now available?

First, of course, external events cannot always be predicted, let alone quantified – using the term 'external' to cover political or industrial crises in this country or overseas. Thus, for example, a 5- or 6-weeks national strike will throw out any calculations perhaps for a year ahead : but no forecasting model in the world can be programmed on the assumption that a national strike will take place in say 10 weeks, will last say 6 weeks, will affect a detailed list of sectors of industry, will be settled on conditions predictable today, and so on.

The second point is more subtle in that it is concerned with the nature of the forecasting exercise and the character of the economic forecasters involved. The more complex a model becomes, the more hard and high level the work involved in formulating the model, the more the emotional commitment of the operators who may tend to become more and more fascinated by the techniques : in this state of commitment it is only too easy to overlook the fact that the raw material, i.e. the statistical material being produced by day-to-day administration, may be at times deficient, and that the necessary mathematical assumptions being made can be dubious.

The point about the raw material being a by-product of other activities has already been made : the mathematical assumptions can be an even more serious fault. At the risk of a vast oversimplification, the great danger is an assumption of economic rationality in the behaviour of the business community – defining economic rationality as having complete knowledge of the economic factors in a situation and then doing what is *economically* in the best interests of the individual making the decision. This economic rationality however is not always a fair assumption, while businessmen may be ill-informed about a situation and their morale may be low after perhaps a series of government measures which are seen as adverse to their interests. The most common example of economically confused action in recent years has been the sort of situation where it would be economically rational to expand production and output, but where businessmen, whose confidence has been shattered, simply refuse to risk doing so, and so throw out the economically sensible calculations. Forecasters and economists are only too liable in this situation to say that it is the businessmen who are wrong, not the forecast. So, in an objective sense, they are but since the businessmen's decisions will effectively determine what does happen there is scant comfort to the public in the idea that reality ought logically to adjust to the forecast and not the forecast to reality.

As a hypothesis it would be interesting to consider to what extent business forecasters relying on econometric models may become detached from reality, in the sense that they may rarely or never meet businessmen whose actions are intuitive rather than rational, and whose interpretations of national economic conditions and the appropriate reaction of business may be very different from their own. The subtle temptation for the forecaster is to try to remedy deficiencies in the statistical raw material by more and more mathematical refinement: it is probably salutary that a forecasting team should contain non-econometricians and even non-economists, possibly social scientists who might be able to explain the (in the forecaster's terms) non-rational behaviour of the business community, which is only too likely to upset the highly mathematical models which have developed in recent years. Certainly it ought to be an imperative for forecasters to meet businessmen rather more often than they do – and on a more official basis.

The Available Short-term Forecasts

There are in the United Kingdom a variety of official, semi-official and independent forecasts and forecasting models. On the official side government departments and public bodies make their forecasts as a necessary preliminary to any meaningful planning of future policy. These forecasts are not in practice published and governments have been rather chary of publishing details for more than a year or two ahead except in very general terms.

Other official forecasts of possibly less political significance are those published by international organisations such as O.E.C.D.

or by the conjunctural committees of E.E.C. They are probably less important in real political terms, but in so far as they are published, or more easily 'leaked' to the press than the highly secure Whitehall figures, they are more readily available for comment or criticism.

At the semi-official level, forecasts such as the quarterly publication of the National Institute for Economic and Social Research give a useful and informed comparison with official forecasts, and perhaps for that reason tend to be received with reverence by economic commentators. University institutions also produce reasonably authoritative forecasts, their authority deriving in part from the intellectual resources available in their preparation, and in part from the forecasters generally having a good entrée to government circles and for that reason being liable to be regarded with considerable care by their official opposite numbers in the forecasting profession.

Finally there are a variety of unofficial forecasts – the monthly *Sunday Telegraph* forecast being the best known example, as well as a few highly skilled commercial research units who exist by selling their forecasts, on subscription, to industry.

It would be comforting to say that the more sophisticated and expensive forecasting techniques used, the more accurate the result would turn out to be. Humiliatingly the forecasts by the small underequipped teams appear to be as good, or as bad, on the average, as the most expensive.

The existence of this type of self-fulfilling prophecy among businessmen which can cause an economy to miss the chance of growth (or alternatively avoid a recession simply because businessmen do not believe a recession will take place) has been commented upon. It is a behavioural rather than an economic concept – although Keynes allowed for the possibility under the concept of expectations – and cannot really be measured by mathematical techniques.

If it is to be measured at all, it has to be done by survey methods, the second of the techniques available. What one is doing is simply asking for opinions, regardless of whether these opinions make exact economic sense. Essentially these surveys involve asking firms how they see their future prospects over the next few months or year : what they see as the main problems and opportunities; whether they are likely to require more or less labour; whether they see costs rising, and if so, by how much.

Such services are really measuring business confidence, and although they are rough and ready compared with the mathematical techniques, they have the advantage of showing how industrialists perceive a situation, not how politicians or economists think they *ought* to perceive the situation.

Once again there are a variety of such surveys, some published, others not, some fairly rigidly structured, others more impressionistic and 'grass roots' in their approach. The *Investment Intentions Survey* of the Department of Trade and Industry or the Confederation of British Industry *Quarterly Survey* of business opinion are possibly the most important published sources, followed closely by the monthly *Financial Times* survey on similar lines. But even the unpublished, and on occasion, unquantified opinion-sounding efforts by trade associations or public authorities provide useful pointers to how and when business confidence grows or wanes.

Such surveys, of course, are far from perfect not least because business sentiment can fluctuate from month to month, and the organisers or the respondents may have their own axes to grind. And, of course, surveys of this nature suffer from the usual weaknesses of any survey of hypothetical opinion, when men or women are being asked for opinions which affect more than their private or family decisions. It is for example one thing to find a businessman willing to express an opinion that he *intends* to increase the level of investment in his company; it is another thing to assume that he will actually do so and to the extent he said when it was an opinion and not a hard-and-fast decision which had to be taken. Opinion is always cheaper and easier than action. Moreover it is not always easy to ensure that a survey, particularly a postal survey with no real commitment, will be filled in by the man who will make the decision. A questionnaire, no matter how dressed up is another form, and form filling is among those activities which tend to get passed down the hierarchy.

In spite of these limitations however there is little doubt that opinion sounding of this nature is one of the best methods presently available of measuring the extent to which the non-rational but self-fulfilling prophecy phenomenon operates in a short-term situation. Certainly reliance on mathematical models alone can be dangerous.

A major characteristic of short-term forecasting is that it can virtually be divorced from forward planning for the simple reason that most actions initiated by the central government will have their major effects outside the timespan of the short-term forecast. Taxes can be cut or raised, expansion may be encouraged or discouraged but the effects are slow in picking up: unless, that is, the action is an emergency clamp-down like a credit squeeze – and even in this instance, while the desired results may appear fairly quickly, the adverse effects will be felt for possibly years.

In medium- or long-term forecasting, by contrast, forecast and forward planning are inextricable: once we are considering a span of years rather than months, then the forecasts depend on the plans which the government is implementing concurrently with the forecast, or has yet to implement. Short-term forecasting produces an assessment of what will happen *unless* certain changes are made (and possibly in spite of any changes made) by the central government: medium- and long-term forecasts are assessments of what will happen depending on what the government does now or in the future.

Medium-term Forecasting

In some respect the task of the medium-term forecaster, looking up to five to seven years ahead, has more pitfalls than that of the short- or long-term forecaster. He is operating in a field of speculation where mathematical projections of existing trends have been pushed beyond an acceptable level, without having reached the point where fairly free speculation on future developments, based on technological breakthrough, can be made without much fear of being disproved.

Possibly for this reason, not many independent workers in the field publish detailed results; in spite of this medium-term forecasts inevitably covering in the five-to-seven-year period at least one general election are clearly important in any political party's electoral strategy.

As has been said, medium-term forecasting covers a span when substantial capital investment can be brought 'into stream', so to speak, as productive capacity. In the context of private industry it covers the period which would be the concern of corporate strategy for those few firms which practise that mystery instead of reacting to events. More realistically in the present context it is the minimum period of practical strategic planning in the public sector, i.e. when forecasts and planning can be meshed together, and when, within the constraints of existing technology, it may be possible to ensure that future reality will correspond with the planned intention.

The extent to which central governments practise medium-term planning (or at least are prepared to publish details of what their expectations are) depends to a large extent on their political colouring, and therefore on their attitude to planning and public sector investment. At the extreme are the communist countries with official five- or seven-year plans. Unfortunately it is difficult to get objective estimates of the extent to which they are fulfilled: clearly however such plans are immensely complex; any delay in the timetable is likely to have a chain reaction throughout the remainder of the life-span of the plan.

The more open societies of the west may also have such plans. When, as almost inevitably happens, they go awry, they are liable to gather for their originators a good deal of scorn, merited or otherwise. There is in the United Kingdom something of a cycle on medium-term planning, namely that an ambitious and overly detailed national plan is launched, gets out of schedule, is amended, then founders amid general scorn. The concept goes underground for a few years until a general feeling emerges that a plan at least gives an objective measure of achievement; at this stage, however, it may be inexpedient from the political point of view to publish any detailed forecasts, which are only too obvious hostages to fortune. Left-wing governments show more enthusiasm about publication, Right-wing governments show more discretion.

The job of the medium-term forecaster is, or ought to be, to block in the possible results of alternative strategies, based on the technology and international political situation existing or likely to exist within the time under discussion. The point about the political situation is important because the fact that estimates go wrong is not in general caused by unforeseen developments in technology, but in external events – the political crisis, the unpredictable political event, the unexpected industrial or political development.

In the mid-1960s who could have confidently predicted that within seven years there would be several outbreaks of war or civil war in sensitive areas of the world; that there would be a discovery of oil and gas in British territorial waters on a scale to affect future developments of the whole energy industry and substantially change the balance-of-payments pattern; or that with the unexpected retirement of President de Gaulle the United Kingdom would become a member of the European Economic Community? All these developments were *possible* when, for example, the Labour government came to power in October 1964: some were even *probable*, but none was literally *predictable*. The fact is that they were not predictable for the period which would have been covered by a medium-term forecast in 1964.

It is probable that any period of five to seven years in the future will be as full of equally dramatic and unpredictable events. The only certainty is that any forecast which assumes no equivalent developments will become rapidly outdated. Detailed predictions which show quarter by quarter detailed and quantifiable projections are merely inviting trouble. Without the rather illusory comforts of mathematical techniques to give an air of precision to his forecasts, the medium-term forecaster quantifies at his peril.

At best then, a medium-term forecast indicates the limit of possible developments on certain planning assumptions. It does not indicate an accurate and, above all, quantifiable judgement.

Long-term Forecasting

This is frankly speculation, accepting as it does that, for the sake of the forecast, virtually any of the present technological constraints can be eliminated, that there will be, if needed, by technological breakthroughs an end to bottlenecks and so forth : in other words that the future can be planned rather than encountered. In real life events, particularly political events, will change the pattern dramatically. Politicians, like industrialists, rarely think more than a few months ahead; they rarely have time to.

Mathematical techniques of projection have virtually no place in such speculation. Indeed they can be positively dangerous if given serious consideration, for the simple reason that to project an existing economic series, e.g. of G.D.P., unemployment, balance-of-payments figures, will within a few years produce an exponential rate of growth or decline, that is to say either the abolition of that particular problem or complete disaster within a generation or two. The flaw in this sort of mathematical projection is that either all other relevant series are held stable, i.e. that except in the area being forecast there is an economic and technological freeze: or alternatively subjective judgements are made about how other series will move, the dubious subjectivity gets buried in sophisticated mathematical techniques and the end results tend to confirm, in an ostensibly objective sort of way, the original assumptions and probably prejudices of the forecaster. There is fortunately some indication that society in general and technology in particular is more resilient than many long-term forecasts would concede. Long-term forecasting in national terms indicates an aim, not the method or prospects of achieving that aim.

Long-term forecasting has a role of indicating problem areas in the future, i.e. of a possible energy gap in the next ten to twenty years, or a dramatic change in population size. But it indicates only one scenario which can be changed in good time if action is taken. Few things are inevitably ordained in a nation's future.

Forecasting – by Whom?

There is thus a substantial difference in principle as well as in techniques between short-term forecasting and medium- and long-term. The further ahead the forecast is to be projected, the more political objectives and therefore deliberate long-range planning determine the forecast result. Thus in the early 1970s one might consider the implications of 5 per cent growth over say two years, without having to go back to first principles and consider whether 5 per cent growth was really desirable. Suppose however one were being asked to forecast the results of twenty years of 5 per cent growth: almost certainly it would make sense to ask whether 5 per cent growth should have an overriding priority for all that time; might it not be better for example to have greater leisure, devote more public funds to improving the environment at the expense of more investment in capital equipment to ensure the 5 per cent growth, abolish poverty among the elderly by diverting resources from growth towards the elderly, or any combination of these desirable aims?

The point is not that an infinite extension of whatever is given priority today is necessarily wrong : perhaps the best use of resources would be to push on for the 5 per cent growth target of the early 1970s, always providing that the various constraints could be neutralised. But clearly there is more room for manoeuvre on a twenty-year scale, and therefore implicitly any forecast on present priorities to the objectives which are set by the community. A forecast on present priorities might suggest an average wage of say £5000 per annum at current prices, another forecast might say that pensioners could be given say £30 weekly at current prices, and so on. Somebody has got to set the priorities, before the forecasters follow.

Such planning and forecasting is, or ought to be, the stuff of party politics in a country like the United Kingdom : it ought to be the task of the politician – or rather the research departments of the major political departments – to at least carry out the preliminary calculations for medium- or long-term planning.

The British situation is by no means universal. In France for example, where planning has enjoyed a degree of prestige and success not noticeable in Britain, much of the impetus comes from the administrative machinery, not the political parties. This situation however owes as much to two or more generations of weak political government, which lasted until the late 1950s. It is doubtful whether it would have been possible for the civil service to have taken on such responsibilities but for the weaknesses of the Third and Fourth Republics, and it is by no means certain that after a decade or two of strong presidential government the planning functions will stay with the civil service.

A second factor which probably operated was the practical inability even of a strong civil service to impose short-term tactical changes, even where these were deemed necessary. In a situation where for example severe economic restraint would have saved the franc from inflation and devaluation, the credit squeeze simply did not work as it would have done in Britain. Perhaps in hindsight this inability to control the long-term trends was beneficial to France in an economic if not in a political sense.

The United Kingdom by contrast has had strong governments – often misguided governments – but nevertheless powerful enough to control Parliament, the Civil Service and industry. Unfortunately however the major political parties have tended to allow their long-term strategy to be overwhelmed by day-to-day detail. It would not be unfair to say that Conservative governments have been excessively pragmatic in economic planning – in curious contrast to their foreign policy which, right or wrong, has shown reasonable consistency since the war; while on the other hand Labour governments have combined political convictions with an incredible vagueness of detail about what their political objectives involved in detail.

Recently the concept of a Central Policy Review Unit, a sort of non-ideological 'think tank', has emerged that is intended to consider specific long-term trends, at leisure so to speak. It is not clear to what extent the C.P.R.U. merely follows up the implication of remits given to it by its political masters, and to what extent it may originate its own studies : but it is by no means certain that it could or should provide overall long-term planning of the sort required.

Arguably one can say that the pragmatic approach of reacting to situations has worked adequately in the past : but British economic performance has not been all that good, because successive governments have not looked beyond the next economic crisis, or at most the next election. As has been said, 'If you don't know where you are going, any road will get you there.'

Governments in power tend to get swamped in day-to-day detail and feel they have enough to cope with on that basis; the Civil Service tends by nature to be relatively cautious, extending existing ideas rather than initiating new ones. Perhaps in a democratic society this is as well if the politicians are to run the Civil Service and not the Civil Service the politicians.

Understandably too, politicians do not like to give hostages to fortune in the shape of long-range published forecasts. In a democratic society however it is hard to see who else ought to be planning and therefore forecasting in the medium to long term. Short-term forecasting, where the political and economic factors are virtually the given, constraints can be left to the statistician, the econometrician or the economist. But for the longer range, when political and economic objectives are the prerequisite, arguably forecasting is too serious a matter to be left to the fore-caster.

Economic Sophistication and Political Reality

Earlier in this chapter the point was made that in the post-war world there have been revolutionary changes in methods of handling economic data, which enabled vast quantities of the raw materials of economic decisions to be processed quickly and to a degree which would have been impossible a generation be-fore. The staggering change in the dimension of information handled and the speed of processing has of course depended upon the development of the computer and its ancillary equip-ment.

In theory then one ought to see an enormous rise not only in the quantity of decision-taking but above all in its quality. No longer ought it to be an intuitive, hit-or-miss affair. Unfortunately the results of decision-making under the new régime of data pro-cessing have not been commensurably dramatic.

The reasons for the relative lag in improvement in the quality of decisions – as evinced for example by the relatively mediocre results of demand management over the last decade – are con-troversial. But one or two propositions can be made. Some of the new techniques are probably fatally flawed in concept, others are the victims of what can only be described as political expediency.

Arguably at least much of the modern quantitative economics or econometrics, as applied to national economic decisions, are leading up a blind alley because they simply cannot produce a reasonable approximation to real-life problems and the way they are solved. In a sense a good deal of work in this field might be likened to a preoccupation by a group of medieval theologians on the issue of the nature of angels, and how many therefore could dance on the point of a needle. Intellectually stimulating and demanding no doubt: carrying remarkable prestige cer-tainly; but of limited practical application to the everyday or even long-term problems of the medieval church. It is possible to construct a model in econometric terms which will demon-strate where a steel plant or a new airport ought to be sited. In-deed it is possible to construct an almost infinite number of such models, merely by varying some of the premises or some of the quantitative values attached to various elements in the equation. The model, or all the models, will be logically unassailable in the sense that there will be no arithmetical errors. But none of them need have any relationship with what is actually done. The politicians do not understand the models : probably indeed they are not even interested in understanding them; and if they had to defend actual decision-making which ran counter to any model, they could frustrate any argument based on an abstruse calculation merely by disputing the premise from which the model started, that some political factors can be quantified and that, even if they could, they had been quantified correctly. A decision on the siting of anything so important as a steel plant or an airport is as likely to turn on the electoral consequences of such a decision on a few marginal constituencies, as upon any economic niceties. And even if the model builder were sufficiently in touch with political realities to build this factor into his equation, he would still have to quantify the factor as it weighed upon the minds of the various individuals involved in the decision, and how effective each individual was in persuading everyone to put a value on his opinion.

If some economic techniques are inherently flawed by their unreal assumptions, there are a series of more down-to-earth techniques which are also to a greater or lesser degree frustrated by political considerations.

Among such techniques, which are probably fundamentally sound but up to the present more promising in potential than results, can be listed such practices as Cost-Benefit Analysis, P.P.B. (Planning, Programming, Budgeting) and related techniques which are intended to facilitate, indeed force, a more rational economic analysis by the decision-makers at national level. Such techniques in essence are attempting to assess the true costs and advantages to the community of proposed courses of action, not merely the immediate financial bills. In effect they force a rational examination of the exact motives for proposed action, alternative ways of achieving the same results, and a constant review of the input of resources and the outputs, both advantageous and disadvantageous, to the community. It is a sad reality that time and again projects arise whose intentions are not clear, whose intentions indeed change, whose costs accelerate apparently inexorably and whose total impact upon the community at

large becomes incalculable. Projects such as Concorde super-
sonic passenger aircraft or the U.C.S. episode which arose out
of an *ad hoc* decision to keep a single shipyard open, provided
they last long enough and cost enough, become sacred cows. They
seem to develop a life of their own whose status owes little or
nothing to their contribution to sociey.

In theory such economic nonsense would never have arisen if a
serious attempt had been made to apply rational costing techniques at a fairly early stage: and again in theory the techniques were available. But they were simply not applied for the
very good reason that political considerations, creditable or
otherwise, were deemed at each crucial point to be more important than long-term economic considerations.

The implication appears to be that many of these techniques
can be applied only when political considerations are relatively
unimportant. Provided projects are relatively small or politically
neutral then the new economic techniques can be applied. But if
political influences in the situation become significant then all
the techniques can do is in part to point out the probable economic
consequences of various courses of actions, not ensure that the
best solution, in economic terms, is adopted.

It is salutary to remember that a generation or two ago the
subject of economics was more familiarly known as Political
Economy. The older title may have been the apter one.

Educating the Politicians

In view of the relative failure of economists to solve national
economic problems, it would be a bold economist who would
claim the right to educate politicians. But in a limited sense at
least it can be said that some attempt is being made to present
economic alternatives in a more comprehensible form, in the
form of financial statements, outlines of public expenditure over
the next few years, and the like. These can be examined in detail
by Select Committees of Parliament, and although the latters'
powers to analyse fully the economic assumptions and reason-
ing behind these statements is limited, the fact that governments
are now tentatively giving such information is likely to make
criticism of political decisions in the economic field more informed and more perceptive. It also has the advantage of limiting the
temptation merely to make debating points the besetting sin of

the more conventional and publicised Parliamentary Debates
and Parliamentary Questions where the level of economics can
best be described as trivial. In the light of the growing com-
plexity, not to say incomprehensibility, of economic decisions by
governments, the effective control of the public purse by
Parliament is likely to depend more and more on perceptive and
persistent questioning of ministers or senior government
officials by economically competent select committee members
than by the more conventional checks of debate on the floor of
the House where economic truths become subordinate to scoring
off political opponents.

CONCLUSION

MARXIST states have a political and economic ideal to which their societies are supposed to be moving. This is the ultimate advent of communism and the withering away of the state. Western states have no such ideal, no apotheosis in which all problems will disappear.

In theory one might argue that this single objective and ideal consummation might give Marxist society an edge over western democracy, although the political cynic might question whether in the first two or three generations of the Marxist drive towards communism there was any sign of the state withering : rather it has flourished and become more pervasive than ever.

If by contrast the western societies seem more aimless in long-term objectives, there is arguably a good deal more flexibility in the responses that can be developed in the intriguingly dynamic future. The immediate danger in a western society, however, is to substitute for the ideal future a bigger and better version of the present. The obverse is of course to imagine that the economic problems of the future are merely continuations of the problems of the present – to imagine for example that because unemployment or inflation preoccupy much economic argument today, they will continue to occupy the centre of the stage indefinitely. It would be as foolish to imagine this as to imagine that somehow the right policy, or the right gimmick, is going to dispose of them overnight once and for all.

Economic problems are always there. Their magnitude may change. Two or three centuries ago, the current twin problems discussed above would have implied starvation for many. If anyone starves today, even in an inflation-ridden society with unused resources of manpower, it is a culpably administrative oversight, not an inevitable concomitant of that society and its problems. The unemployed today enjoy a standard and quality of life which in many respects would have seemed utopian to the skilled worker of a century ago : it is equally possible that what are seen as the anxieties of the twenty-first century would be mere cavilling at trifles to today's workers. Just as today what we regard as hardship in the United Kingdom would be unimaginable luxury for that part of the world population who live on the edge of literal starvation.

Unless western society heads for a catastrophe, and that would be a catastrophe involving the whole world, rich and poor, east and west alike, affluence is likely to spread, with possibly more and more emphasis on the quality of life and less and less emphasis on the material side.

It is impossible to give an ideal recipe for a better Britain in economic terms, even if one can express this in economic terms alone. But it is difficult to avoid the obvious conclusion that whatever ideals we may choose to aim for in the closing years of the century, their realisation would be made easier if the United Kingdom could secure faster sustained growth. Virtually every other economic problem yields to the application of more resources, and most of our immediate problems arise out of inadequate resources to tackle all problems on an adequate scale. More and more material production does not solve ultimate problems, but only a fool or a saint would assume that they did not matter. Most British people are in neither of these categories, and if they are to have the ability to choose how to mould their future, then faster growth and more resources are an obvious prerequisite. If therefore this book has a theme it is that the relative failure of the British economy to match growth with other countries at the same state of development is a major source of our present problems. And that if we can analyse why, in economic, political, or social terms, we find it difficult to get faster growth, then we are in a far better position, if not to solve all the others, at least to moderate them to the point where they are no longer front-page issues.

INDEX

227

national expenditure 10–14, 46
national income 10–12, 47
National Institute of Economic and Social Research (N.I.E.S.R.) 212
national insurance contributions 197
national output 47
national product 10–12, 13–15
nationalised industries 26
negative income tax 154, 200
'New Deal' 63
non-economic motives 45
North Sea oil 216
Northern Ireland 167

oil prices 164, 185
'on the shelf' projects 115
Organisation for Economic Cooperation and Development (O.E.C.D.) 211
overtime as a means of raising wage rate 118

parliamentary questions 223
Pay Board 180, 184
pay claims 128
pensions see transfer payments
peripheral regions 110, 138
planned obsolescence 39
planning (French pattern) 218
Planning Programme Budgeting (P.P.B.) 221
pool of unemployed 107
Population Census 105
Price Commission 180, 184
private sector 26
productive capacity 81 et seq., 179, 189
propensity see marginal propensity

public sector 26, 52, 64, 88, 93
purchasing power 22

rationing 204
raw material prices 94
reflation 57
Regional Employment Premium (R.E.P.) 134, 138
regional policy 50, 132 et seq.
regulator 196
retail prices see Index of Retail Prices
retirement early to increase employment 119
Roosevelt, President Franklin D. 155

savings 10, 13 et seq.
Scotland 136, 182
seasonally adjusted statistical series 101, 170, 190
Second World War 64
Select Committees (of Parliament) 222
Selective Employment Tax (S.E.T.) 118
self-fulfilling prophecies 17, 113, 212
'Social Contract' 187
standard of living 90 et seq.
Sterling Area 156
sterling Pre-1914 61
'stickiness' of economic change 49
stocks 25, 39
stop–go 65, 68, 90, 149, 157
strikes 129
Suez 65
Sunday Telegraph 212
surplus budgeting 29

taxation 26 et seq., 52, 195,